WITH MALICE AFORETHOUGHT

Sixteen cases of premeditated murder

Also by Georgina Lloyd and published by Bantam Books

One was not Enough
Motive to Murder
The Evil that Men Do

With Malice Aforethought

Sixteen cases of premeditated murder

GEORGINA LLOYD

BANTAM BOOKS

NEW YORK • TORONTO • LONDON • SYDNEY • AUCKLAND

WITH MALICE AFORETHOUGHT

A BANTAM BOOK 0 553 40273 0

Originally published in Great Britain by Robert Hale Ltd.

PRINTING HISTORY
Robert Hale edition published 1989
Bantam edition published 1990

This book is set in Palatino

Bantam Books are published by Transworld Publishers Ltd.,
61–63 Uxbridge Road, Ealing, London W5 5SA,
in Australia by Transworld Publishers (Australia) Pty. Ltd.,
15–23 Helles Avenue, Moorebank, NSW 2170, and in New
Zealand by Transworld Publishers (N.Z.) Ltd., Cnr. Moselle
and Waipareira Avenues, Henderson, Auckland.

Printed and bound in Great Britain by
BPCC Hazell Books
Aylesbury, Bucks, England
Member of BPCC Ltd.

Contents

Contents

Introduction

The notion of premeditated murder, for whatever cause, rarely fails to arouse strong emotions. These may not, however, necessarily be feelings of disgust or revulsion.

The majority of premeditated murders are committed with true 'malice aforethought': murders for gain, multiple killings for sexual gratification, planned elimination of a spouse in order to free a man to marry a mistress, or a woman to wed a lover of long-standing when her recalcitrant husband refuses her a divorce.

What is the solution to these cases as far as the courts are concerned? Obviously these murderers cannot be let loose in society. Life imprisonment seems the right answer for those who kill for gain, for the elimination of an unwanted spouse, or a business rival, and so on. Incarceration in prison, however, is not the way to deal with multiple murderers who kill for the sake of killing – in other words, for pleasure – or for sexual motives. These people are mentally unstable, even if they are not legally insane. They need treatment in a *secure* hospital without any opportunity of escape, perhaps to commit more murders. Neither should they ever be released on parole if there is still even a slight chance that their condition has not been completely cured and their homicidal tendencies eliminated.

No one doctor should be asked to bear the fearful responsibility of returning such a person into society. At least half a dozen experts, acting independently, should assess the patient over a protracted period of time before conferring as a panel on the advisability or otherwise of parole, after which strict supervision should be maintained for a considerable time. For example, when the patient is ordered to see his parole officer at stated intervals, then he *must* do so, and if he does not attend the appointment the authorities must find out why. If a specific residential or job condition is imposed, the parolee must *not* be allowed to change it without express permission and prior approval of the new abode or job by the authorities. Flagrant infringement of the conditions laid down should involve revocation of parole.

Only then can the public feel safe when a capital offender is released into society, while at the same time he is encouraged, after medical and psychiatric treatment, to live a normal life among his fellow human beings. And we, as fellow human beings, owe him the chance to reinstate himself, provided that he keeps the laws which exist for his and our protection.

Georgina Lloyd

1

If They could only Talk

Kidnapping for ransom is about as premeditated as you can get. And when it is followed by murder, it can only be described as calculated, callous and cold-blooded.

The kidnapping for ransom and murder of Mrs Muriel McKay in 1969 was the first crime of this kind with an adult victim in British criminal history. It was also only the third case in fifty years in which a murder conviction was obtained without the victim's body ever being found.

Muriel McKay was the wife of Alexander (known as Alick) McKay, a national newspaper executive, who at sixty was five years older than his wife. Both were Australian. They lived in a large detached house in Wimbledon, London, where they were known to neighbours and friends alike as a happy family who enjoyed an idyllic marriage enlivened by frequent visits from their married children who had families of their own. They liked entertaining, led a rewarding social life and also spent time in fund-raising for charity.

Alick McKay, on coming to London, from Australia, had obtained a position as advertisement director in the *Daily Mirror* newspaper group. He continued to prosper in his chosen career, becoming the advertisement director of the newly formed International Publishing Company in 1963. Two years later he was awarded a CBE. Then, in 1969, Rupert Murdoch gained control of the publishing group – often referred to as 'the Murdoch empire' – and offered Alick McKay a job as deputy chairman of the *News of the World*.

Not long after his new appointment he found himself in the role of temporary acting chairman while Rupert Murdoch and his attractive young wife, who were also Australian, decided to go home for a six-week holiday.

Alick McKay, left in charge as from 19 December 1969, was given the use of the company car, a dark blue Rolls Royce. Using this car indirectly led to the death of his wife, but he had no way of knowing this at the time.

Some years previously, two brothers, Arthur and Nizamodeen Hosein, had arrived in Britain from Trinidad. Arthur, the elder of the two, was obsessed with fantasies of becoming a country squire. In his tailoring business in London's East End, he had the reputation of being somewhat eccentric. He earned good money and was able to send a substantial sum home each week to his family in Trinidad. Had he nurtured normal ambitions to improve his business and expand, he could have quite likely ended up owning a chain of tailoring businesses. But this was apparently not enough to satisfy his vanity: he wanted to be a country gentleman, no less. So he decided to purchase a farm in Hertfordshire on mortgage and declared to all and sundry his driving ambition 'to become a millionaire'.

This fantasy world did not appeal to Nizamodeen (known as Nizam), who lacked the outgoing, jovial *bonhomie* of his older brother. When Arthur moved into the farmhouse he bought stock and hired his brother as a low-paid farm labourer and stockman. Nizam dutifully gave up his technical college studies. It was not long, however, before he was complaining that a low agricultural wage plus his keep was not getting him anywhere. He berated his brother, asking him where all the wealth and social life his new lifestyle was supposed to have brought him was? The introverted Nizam was far more realistic than Arthur, and realized that between his brother's extravagant aspirations and the reality of being accepted by the gentry was a gulf he was unlikely to bridge just by rearing a few prize herds of pedigree animals. To use the popular phrase, a 'get rich quick' scheme was needed.

The answer to Arthur's dreams came to him one night as the two brothers were watching a television show. David Frost was interviewing Rupert Murdoch, and during the interview Murdoch revealed that he was a multi-millionaire. The amount of money mentioned in connection with the Murdoch takeover bid for the *News of the World* was fantastic. It clearly made a terrific impression on Arthur. 'All that money for a newspaper!' he kept saying to himself.

Then he turned to Nizam. 'Do you realize what this means?' he said. 'This man Murdoch is a multi-millionaire, and his wife is a real looker. If someone kidnapped her, he would surely part with one of his millions just to get her back. And that someone might just as well be *us*!'

'You're crazy,' said Nizam.

'I'd be crazy if I didn't take up an opportunity like that!' retorted Arthur. 'Let's get down to business and plan the operation right now!'

After some persuasion, Nizam gradually veered towards the view that the proposed kidnap of Mrs Murdoch might not be as difficult as it had at first sounded. First the brothers would have to do a bit of reconnoitring; then, when they were ready, Arthur would have to ensure that Else, his German wife, would go and spend an extended Christmas holiday in Germany with her parents. That would not be any problem, since she did that every year anyway.

From 30 October, the date of the David Frost interview, until 13 December, when Else Hosein left for Germany with the couple's children, the two brothers did little more than talk about their bizarre plan. After this date they swung into action. They looked up Rupert Murdoch in the telephone directory and tried Directory Enquiries, but without success: the newspaper magnate had an unlisted number. They consulted *Kelly's Street Directory* with an equal lack of success. Then they drove to the offices of the *News of the World* in Bouverie Street, off Fleet Street, and snooped around in the staff car park where they spotted a dark blue Rolls Royce, with the licence plate number ULO 18F. Who else but the chairman would own such a car? But first they must check to be sure that their surmise was correct: they did not want to waste time on a wild-goose chase.

Nizam was detailed to call at the offices of the GLC at County Hall where, using a false name, he told the girl clerk in the vehicle registration department that he was anxious to trace the owner of a Rolls Royce ULO 18F. He said, he had had a slight collision with the car and needed this information for insurance purposes: 'I don't think the driver realized I had scraped most of the paint off his offside bumper – he just drove on,' he added convincingly. The girl could tell him only that the vehicle in question was owned by the *News of the World*. This confirmed the brothers' supposition about the ownership of the car.

There now remained the problem of finding out where Rupert Murdoch and his wife lived. The best way to do this, the brothers reasoned, would be to follow the Rolls in their own car from Fleet Street to its destination in the evening. Just before Christmas they did so, entirely oblivious of the fact that Mr and Mrs Murdoch had left for their holiday in Australia, and that the passenger in the back of the chauffeured Rolls was his deputy, Alick McKay. They did not see McKay's face, since he was well-muffled against the December chill in fur-lined greatcoat, cashmere scarf and hat. The car led them through London to the suburb of Wimbledon and pulled up outside 20 Arthur Road. 'An omen!' cried Arthur Hosein as the younger man skilfully turned the car around and they headed back home to Rook's Farm, near the village of Stocking Pelham. They would now be able to get down to the nitty-gritty of planning the kidnap of – as they thought – Mrs Murdoch and demand a ransom for her return of one million pounds.

On Monday, 29 December, after returning home from a Christmas holiday spent with his daughter and son-in-law in Sussex, Alick McKay set out for his office in the chauffeur-driven Rolls Royce, at about 9.30 a.m. His wife waved goodbye from the front door. Little did he know that he would never see her again.

Mrs McKay, equally unaware of her impending fate, busied herself about the kitchen, preparing food for the evening meal; she then went out to the shops, to the bank, to a shoe-repairer's and to a boutique, where she bought a dress with matching coat. Back at home she prepared a light lunch for herself prior to leaving in her own car, a Ford Capri, for a routine check-up with her Wimpole Street dentist. She bought the evening papers, put the car away, made a cup of tea and settled down to read the papers in her favourite armchair by the fire in the lounge. Her pet dog lay at her feet. The time by now was about 5.40 p.m. She switched on the television to watch the early evening news.

The news was in progress when the front door bell rang. This was heard by an independent witness. At about 6 p.m. a neighbour, Mrs Lydiatt, was walking past the house when she noticed a dark-coloured car parked in the drive. She also spotted that the hall light was on; this could be seen through a glass panel above the front door.

At 7.45 p.m. Alick McKay returned from work. After dismissing the chauffeur, as the Rolls receded into the distance he discovered to his alarm that the front door was unlocked. This was most unlike his wife; she never left the door unlocked. With a vague sense of misgiving he entered the house, and immediately knew that something was seriously amiss. The telephone had been ripped from the wall and lay on the floor; his wife's reading spectacles also lay nearby and her handbag lay on the stairs, its contents scattered. Curiously, there were some other items scattered around, which he did not recognize as belonging to the house: a ball of string, a tin of wide sticking plaster, and a billhook with a wooden handle. The dog lay dozing before the fire, but there was no sign of his wife. Nor was there any note left saying she had popped out. Normally she was always there when he came home from work with a warm welcome and a meal cooking.

Alick McKay wasted no time. He telephoned the police from a neighbour's house. Frankly they were puzzled. While Fleet Street had a scoop on its own doorstep, the police, who openly considered that the attentions of the Press were a nuisance, were wondering whether the lady's apparent disappearance was just a publicity stunt to revive flagging circulations. They thought that Alick McKay seemed strangely calm, and even ventured the opinion, no doubt covertly among themselves, that he might be involved. They then considered the hypothesis that Mrs McKay might have left of her own accord, perhaps involved with another man. This theory was scotched as preposterous by all who knew the couple.

The next theory was that there had been a family

disagreement and that Mrs McKay had gone to stay with a relative or friend for a few days. Alick McKay was able to convince the police that such an idea was, to use his words, 'utter rubbish'. However, all these fancy theories were very soon to be discounted, for at 1.15 a.m. that same night a call came through on the McKays' telephone, which had been reconnected.

By this time the family's two married daughters and their husbands had arrived, along with several friends. One person had to man the telephone at all times while a policeman manned the extension in the kitchen. The 1.15 a.m. call was taken by David Dyer, one of the McKays' sons-in-law.

'This is M3 of the Mafia. I want to speak to Mr McKay.' Colour drained from Alick McKay's face as he took the receiver in silence. A hush fell on the roomful of police and others. Detective Sergeant White picked up the receiver of the extension in the kitchen.

'We are from the Mafia. I am M3. We have your wife and we want a million pounds by Wednesday.'

'This is ridiculous!' was the reply. 'I haven't got a million!'

'Then you'd better get it,' said the voice. 'You have a lot of rich friends. Get it from them. We tried to get Rupert Murdoch's wife. We couldn't get her, so we took your wife instead. You have a million by Wednesday night or we will kill her.'

'What do I have to do?' asked McKay.

'All you have to do is to get the money and wait for us to contact you. Have the money or you won't have a wife.'

The family, though horrified, was relieved that Mrs McKay was apparently still alive in the hands of a lunatic gangster. However, the call had lasted long enough to enable it to be traced to a public telephone box in Epping, Essex. The police found it hard to believe that a kidnapper would make a ransom demand from a public telephone box since it could so easily be traced. Then, too, the claim to be a member of the Mafia was very far-fetched. 'Mafia M3' sounded more like something out of an American movie. The police thought the whole thing must be an elaborate hoax.

While McKay thought that the intense Press publicity

would help his wife's safe return, the police were less than convinced of this. And while the *Sun* blazed a banner headline, 'Mystery of Press Chief's Missing Wife' across its front page on Tuesday, 30 December, the police were still taking the view that McKay knew more about the whole affair than he was admitting. As far as they were concerned, he was still the prime suspect. The house was searched from top to bottom, as was the garden, much to the annoyance of the family. The police were in fact pursuing their inquiries in various quarters.

A description of the missing woman was issued and circulated, and a Press conference was held in which details of the one million pound ransom demand were revealed. As statements, alleged sightings and other leads began to pour in, an incident control point was set up at Wimbledon police station. Friends and neighbours of the McKays were questioned, and the clue of the 'dark-coloured car' seen by Mrs Lydiatt was followed up. Round the clock two policemen were stationed inside the house and two outside. A tape-recording device was plugged into the McKays' telephone. Hoax calls were made frequently, which only tended to reinforce police opinion that the whole thing was a publicity stunt. McKay was naturally very annoyed at this slur on his integrity, as was the rest of the family.

At 4.56 p.m. on Tuesday, the man who called himself M3 rang again from a telephone box; David Dyer, who took the call, distinctly heard the pips. 'Your wife has just posted a letter to you,' the voice said. 'Are you going to co-operate? If you value your wife's life, do not bring in the police. We have been following you. Did you get our message? Have you got the money?' There was a click as the caller rang off.

There were still no instructions as to how or where the money was to be delivered. That night McKay's daughter Diane, the wife of David Dyer, appealed on the BBC television news for her mother's safe return and for the kidnapper, wherever he might be, to drop his preposterous ransom demands. 'Just return my mother safely,' she concluded, 'and we will not turn you in to the police.' Naturally the police were furious. Whether Mrs McKay were returned safely or not, kidnapping and blackmail

were crimes and punishable by law. Subsequent to the
broadcast there was an increase in the nuisance calls,
which infuriated the police even more.

The following morning a letter arrived for McKay
postmarked Tottenham, N17. Mrs McKay had written:
'Please do something to get me home. I am blindfolded. It
is very cold here ... I have only two blankets ... Please
co-operate, for I cannot keep going ... What have I done to
deserve this? Love, Muriel.' The handwriting was verified
as authentically hers. The police decided to keep the
contents of the letter secret, but somehow they were
leaked to the *Sun* and to the Press Association, and most
dailies carried the text in full. The police were seething.

Diane made another appeal on television, this time on
ITN news. Police or no police, the family felt that they had
rights too in trying to rescue their mother, even though
their methods clashed with those of the police. After all, as
the family pointed out, the police had neither rescued her
nor caught the kidnapper yet.

On the evening of Thursday, 1 January 1970, M3 called
again. This time the call was untraceable: it had been made
on the STD system. Diane answered the call, but M3 did
not want to talk to her, and rang off. Minutes later he was
back. 'Tell them I'll contact them tomorrow and they've
got to get a million pounds, all in fives and tens. That's it.'

'Where on earth do I get a million pounds?' queried
Diane.

'That's not my business,' M3 replied before ringing off.

Nine days elapsed, and nothing more was heard from
the mysterious M3. By this time the police, the press and
the family all believed that Mrs McKay had genuinely
been kidnapped. But who could the kidnapper be? A man
who claimed to be a member of the Mafia and who
demanded a million-pound ransom? And why was he
doing this? Was he someone who had a grudge against the
News of the World? Perhaps a drug dealer who had been
exposed in its pages, and was out for revenge?

In desperation Alick McKay asked the police for
permission to appeal himself on television, and they had
no choice but to allow him to do so. In his appeal he asked
for proof that his wife was still alive. The result of this was
that a person purporting to be M3 wrote to the editor of

the *News of the World* stating that for days he had been unable to get through to the McKay house owing to the continual jamming of the telephone line with other calls. His instructions were that the million pound ransom was to be delivered in two instalments, and that details would follow.

Four days later M3 rang both the editor of the *News of the World* and the McKay house. Alick McKay took the call.

'You co-operate,' the voice said, 'and you'll get your wife back.' Then he rang off. By now the police, who had been carefully examining the accent on the tape-recordings made of his calls, were convinced that he was a coloured man, possibly of West Indian origin.

Alick McKay was, understandably, in a tense emotional state by this time. It was he who took M3's next call, on the afternoon of Monday, 19 January. 'Bring a gun and shoot me!' he cried, 'and stop making these impossible demands. I haven't got a million pounds. It's ridiculous even to talk about it. I can't give you what I haven't got!'

'If you don't co-operate,' replied M3, 'you alone will be responsible if you never see your wife again.'

'What have I done to deserve this?'

'I don't know,' replied the voice, 'but I'm very sorry we have to do this because your wife is such a nice person.'

'I can get you twenty thousand pounds, but I'll need some time,' McKay said.

'That's not enough. It must be half a million, first delivery.'

'Take me instead!' McKay cried. M3 rang off, and McKay collapsed sobbing into a chair.

The police now persuaded Ian McKay, Alick's son, to take all calls to lessen the stress upon his father. Two days later M3 called again, saying that two letters were on their way. These, with a ransom demand with detailed instructions, postmarked Wood Green, N22, arrived on Thursday, 22 January. In one letter Mrs McKay referred to her daughter's television appeal, which she had apparently seen, or at least heard. She wrote, 'My health and spirits are deteriorating ... excuse handwriting, it is so cold here and I'm blindfolded. Please co-operate with the gang. The earlier you get the money the sooner I can come home. Please keep the police out of it if you want to see me alive ...'

The accompanying note told McKay to put half a million pounds in fives and tens into a black suitcase and bring it, in his wife's Ford Capri, to a telephone box on the corner of Church Street and Cambridge Road in Edmonton at 10 p.m. on 1 February: there he would receive further instructions.

The following day M3 rang three times to confirm that the letters and the demand had been received, and to repeat his threats. The calls were taken by Ian McKay. Ian demanded further proof that his mother was alive, and on the following Monday further communication was received enclosing two more letters from Mrs McKay and also three pieces of material cut from clothes she was known to have been wearing when she was abducted.

Wads of imitation money were made up by the police, an electronic tracking device was attached to a black suitcase, and two police officers, impersonating the chauffeur and McKay, drove the Rolls to the pick-up point. This took them along the A10. Lying in ambush at various points along the route were more than 150 police officers in 50 unmarked police cars.

From one telephone box to another the two officers were guided by M3 with part-instructions until at length they reached a place known as Dane End, High Cross, where the suitcase was to be left. At precisely midnight this was done, and the Rolls headed back to London. But the trap failed. So many police were driving about, some thinly disguised as Hell's Angels on powerful motorbikes, that they unwittingly blew their own cover and the kidnappers panicked. One CID man logged five police vehicles to every private car that passed him on the stretch of road he was monitoring. Small wonder that the operation was a dismal failure.

What the police did not know was that one of these private cars, a Volvo, was being driven by the Hosein brothers. They drove slowly past the suitcase to a transport café where they parked and discussed their next move over coffee. Two plain-clothes detectives happened to pull in for a coffee after them, and gave the game away by discussing the operation in loud voices. The Hoseins fled back to Rook's Farm, eight miles away.

There were to be two more re-runs of the drop

operation, this time without the overkill of dozens of police officers and cars to alarm the kidnappers. M3, indignant at having almost fallen into a police trap, from that point onwards refused to deal with any member of the family but Alick. Meanwhile, Hertfordshire police had been asked to inquire whether any West Indians or other black men lived in the area around where the drop had been made. They said that they believed that two Pakistanis owned a farm near Stocking Pelham. Detectives went to Rook's Farm and found that the alleged Pakistanis were in fact two Muslim brothers from Trinidad named Hosein. The detectives gave the excuse that they were checking on all cars in the area looking for stolen cars. The Hoseins owned two, a Morris Minor and a Volvo. The registration numbers of their cars were filed, among others, at operations headquarters.

The brothers, quite undeterred by apparent police interest in them and doubtless confident of the outcome of their plan, continued the calls. This time Alick McKay, accompanied by Diane, was told to make the drop. A policeman and a policewoman resembling the two McKays in build and general appearance were detailed to dress in their clothes and drive the Rolls. This time another officer was hidden in the back of the big car.

M3 made his final call to the house at 3.30 p.m. on Friday, 6 February. Ian McKay answered it. 'They're on their way,' he said.

A police officer, concealed in a hedge near the drop point, saw a dark blue Volvo, with the registration XGO 994G, slow as it passed the suitcases. The driver seemed to take much more interest in them than did the drivers of other passing cars. Thirty minutes later the Volvo returned, passed the cases, then did a U-turn and passed the cases again. Just at that moment a bingo hall was disgorging a large crowd of people who were going home after the last game. The Volvo gathered speed and drove off.

Some time later the Volvo reappeared and drove slowly past the suitcases. By this time the policeman hiding in the hedge was probably feeling decidedly cramped – and hungry and wished the whole thing would come to an end so that he could go home; the time was 10.47 p.m.

At 11 p.m. a public-spirited couple named Abbott saw the unattended suitcases and thought someone must have forgotten them while going for petrol at the nearby garage. The wife stood guard over the cases while the husband rang the local police station to report their find. An officer duly came and took the cases to the police station, where the duty officer, opening them to seek identification, nearly fell off his chair at seeing half a million pounds. He did not, of course, realize that the money was fake and had itself been made up by police.

The operation to catch M3 was abandoned at 11.40 p.m. Back at the house in Wimbledon, the family was becoming more and more depressed. Failure again. The McKays made coffee and sandwiches and gathered to discuss the latest events. Sleep was impossible.

At 3 a.m. a visitor arrived. It was a police officer to report that the sighting of the Volvo had tallied with other entries in the crime files at operations headquarters. 'We think we may be on to them,' he said simply.

At 8 a.m. on the Saturday morning a large detachment of police visited Rook's Farm. They observed the suspect Volvo parked outside. Arthur Hosein cheerfully invited the officers in. 'Is it about my car?' he said affably. 'I do not deal in stolen property: I do not need to.' The officers asked for permission to search the house. 'You can search where you like,' Arthur replied. 'You won't find any stolen car parts here.'

What they did find, however, was an exercise-book with some pages torn out. Forensic examination later revealed that the torn edges dovetailed exactly into the torn edges of the lined paper on which Mrs McKay had written her desperate letters. They also found a tin of sticking plaster similar to the one found in the McKay house, a billhook like the one found there, and a sawn-off shotgun. Asked about the shotgun, Arthur said that he used it on the farm for shooting vermin and rabbits. 'You don't use a *sawn-off* shotgun for such uses,' the officer pointed out. Hosein did not reply.

One of the officers identified Nizam as the man who had driven the Volvo the previous night. At least some good had come of his uncomfortable sojourn in the hedge. The brothers were driven to London for further questioning and the Volvo was taken in for forensic examination. Fingerprints from the car were identical to those found on the ransom demand notes and the envelopes in which they had been posted.

On Tuesday, 10 February 1970, Arthur and Nizamodeen Hosein were charged with the abduction and suspected murder of Mrs Muriel McKay. Handwriting experts were agreed that Arthur had written the ransom demands, and voice experts decided that Nizam had made most of the M3 calls. Neither of the two said anything incriminating. Arthur, still his usual voluble self, hardly stopped talking; Nizam, however, hardly said a word. On two occasions he made a half-hearted attempt to kill himself while in custody. 'Arthur is always getting me into trouble!' he complained. It was plain that he had always been dominated by his brother.

While on remand they appeared no fewer than seventeen times in Wimbledon Magistrates' Court pending extensive inquiries by the police over a seven-month period, during which they searched Rook's Farm from end to end and scoured the vicinity for clues. Not a trace of Mrs McKay could be found.

Charged with murder, kidnapping and blackmail, the Hosein brothers were brought to trial at the Old Bailey on Monday, 14 September 1970 before Mr Justice Sebag Shaw. The Attorney-General, Sir Peter Rawlinson, led for the Crown; Arthur was defended by Barry Hudson QC, and Nizam by Douglas Draycott QC. It was 6 October before the trial ended. The Hoseins' father came from Trinidad to attend the trial along with the entire McKay family and Arthur's wife Else. Both brothers were found guilty on all charges, the jury recommending leniency in the case of Nizam. When asked if he had anything to say, Arthur shouted, 'Injustice has not only been done, it has also been seen to be done!' He also added a statement that implied that he thought the judge to be biased against black people.

Both brothers were sentenced to life imprisonment on the murder charge; Arthur was also given twenty-five years on the other charges, and Nizam fifteen years. Both appealed, but the appeals were dismissed.

Only the Hosein brothers know what happened to Mrs

McKay, and they are not talking – not even the loquacious Arthur. There are unconfirmed reports of the sound of a shotgun being fired at the farm some time around the beginning of January 1970, and of an acrid smell of burning coming from the direction of the farm on or after 6 January. The police tend to support the most prevalent rumour in the area, that Mrs McKay was drugged, shot and her body fed to the pigs after dismemberment. It would certainly have been difficult to hide her at the farm after the return from Germany of Else and the children.

A pedigree herd of seven Wessex Saddleback pigs had been kept at Rook's Farm. By the time the police raided the farm the boar and four of the sows had been sold and slaughtered, leaving two sows and their litters. Mrs Hosein did not sell these until 26 February. It was known that Mrs McKay had been taking cortisone, a prescribed drug, for a skin condition. No one thought to examine the pigs for the presence of this steroid in their tissues, which would have ensued had they consumed any parts of a body containing cortisone.

If they could only talk!

2

'Excuse Fingers'

Major Herbert Rowse Armstrong was a solicitor, and has the dubious distinction of being the only solicitor in British criminal history ever to be hanged for murder. He was in partnership in the pretty Welsh border town of Hay-on-Wye, in Brecknock on the border with Herefordshire. When the senior partner died in April 1914, the solicitors' practice became Major Armstrong's as the sole partner, and accordingly he had the brass plate on the door changed to read 'H. Rowse Armstrong, Solicitor and Notary Public, Clerk to the Justices'. His practice, however, was destined to bring him little reward, for in November 1914 he enlisted in the Royal Engineers (he received his commission in 1916) and after the cessation of hostilities he remained in the Territorial Army until May 1920, when he was demobbed.

Major Armstrong's wife Katherine (née Friend), whom he had married in 1907, was four years younger than he was. The couple owned a large house called Mayfield in a nearby village known as Cusop Dingle. They had two daughters and a son, and Mrs Armstrong was, not unnaturally, somewhat nervous about her children's future during the war years. In 1917 she made a will leaving everything to them in equal shares, with just a tiny annuity for her husband.

Two months after he left the Army and returned to his practice, the Major's attention began to wander and he started to see a widow named Marion Gale, who lived with her mother at Ford Cottage in Christchurch. He had met her when his Army unit had been posted to the Bournemouth area. Now, renewing the friendship, he reinforced it with dinner and theatre outings, and shortly afterwards the widow became his mistress.

At about this time, Mrs Armstrong's health began to deteriorate. She had never been robust, and her chronic indigestion, rheumatism and neuritis had impelled her to seek relief in a number of homoeopathic remedies (more than fifty bottles of these substances were found in her bedroom after her death). Her mental state, too, began to take a turn for the worse. She had always been somewhat crotchety and domineering, but now her despotism became much more severe. She ruled her husband, her children and her home like an autocrat. A teetotaller herself, she allowed no alcohol in the house, even for offering to guests. The Major was not allowed to smoke his pipe at home, nor was the family allowed to wear anything but carpet slippers indoors. The gramophone was not allowed to be played on Sundays, nor flowers or pot plants kept in the house. With all these petty restrictions, some might think it small wonder that the Major sought consolation elsewhere. He was too shy and peace-loving to stand up to his wife's domination, particularly as he knew that thwarting her might aggravate her physical and mental symptoms.

At this time a new will surfaced, which purported to have been made by Mrs Armstrong, but subsequent investigation proved that the document was in her husband's handwriting, not hers, and that the witnesses – a housekeeper and a maid – had invalidated it by not having signed it simultaneously in the testatrix's presence. In other words, the will was a forgery. The will left everything to her husband and made no provision for her children at all. This in itself was suspicious, since it was well-known that Mrs Armstrong was very attached to all her children.

As her mental state deteriorated, it became clear that she was suffering from an extreme degree of paranoia. She had delusions, heard non-existent voices and footsteps, and imagined intruders. She accused herself of defrauding tradesmen and underpaying the servants, and was amazed when they told her that she was quite mistaken. Doctors and friends of the family were consulted, and after Sunday dinner on 22 August 1920 a conference was held at which it was decided that the best course of action would be to have Mrs Armstrong admitted to a private mental hospital (in those days called an 'asylum'). Mrs Armstrong, it seems, must have agreed, because she was present at this family conference along with her husband, her sister and her niece, and the family solicitor. The requisite forms were signed, and Mrs Armstrong was driven to Barnwood House Hospital, in Gloucester.

No sooner was his wife out of the house than Major Armstrong was free to indulge in such hitherto undreamed-of luxuries as a glass of wine after dinner and the comfort of his pipe as he sat by the fireside in his favourite armchair. He also took frequent trips to London, where his enjoyment was of a less innocuous kind. Soon afterwards he was paying the price: a lengthy course of treatment for syphilis.

In January 1921 the Major entered into a correspondence with the hospital superintendent about the possibility of his wife being allowed to come home. While her physical condition had improved, her mental condition was certainly not normal, and in fact some of her delusions had increased – she had even acquired a few new ones. The superintendent therefore considered that Mrs Armstrong was not yet ready to go home. When the Major persisted, the superintendent thought it rather odd, considering how relieved he had seemed to be when his wife had been admitted. On balance, however, Dr Townsend, the superintendent, realized that the husband's request could not be reasonably denied; after all, he had adequate help in the house with a cook, a maid and a housekeeper and the children. Mrs Armstrong herself also wished to return home. So, brushing off his misgivings, Dr Townsend signed her release.

What Dr Townsend did not know was that the Major had suddenly developed an unseasonal interest in his garden. On 11 January 1921 he purchased a quarter-pound of arsenic from Mr John Davies, the main chemist in Hay-on-Wye. Naturally he had to sign the poisons book and when asked why he wanted such a large quantity he replied that it was to be made up into weedkiller for his large garden, which was overrun with dandelions. When Mr Davies mentioned that it was a bit early in the year to be thinking of killing weeds, the Major said that he wanted to get the job done before his wife came home from the hospital, because afterwards he would not have the time, being occupied with looking after the invalid.

The Major found that, with the demands of his legal practice, a nurse would have to come in to help Mrs Armstrong with dressing, baths, etc., which in her weakened state she still found difficult. The first nurse lasted only four days, unnerved by her charge's constant reference to suicide. Another older and more experienced mental nurse was then engaged. The family doctor, who looked in regularly, was puzzled by the symptoms complained of by the invalid. Although she stayed in bed most of the time, she sometimes ventured downstairs to see how the servants were coping with the household tasks which had formerly always been under her direct supervision. She told the doctor that when she took any steps she had the feeling of 'walking on springs'. The doctor shook his head and looked very thoughtful. 'Very peculiar indeed,' he observed, and he wondered whether it was just the delusion of a mentally-unbalanced woman, or ...?

On Sunday, 13 February, five days after her forty-eighth birthday, a crisis developed. Mrs Armstrong was stricken with muscular spasms and pains, accompanied by vomiting. It was thought that she had contracted a chill from sitting out in the garden, despite the fact that she had been muffled in a down quilt with two hot-water bottles. Dr Thomas Hincks, the thoughtful family GP, thought it most odd that anyone would have allowed a sick woman to sit out in the garden in the middle of February, quilt and hot-water bottles or not. Apparently she had been left sitting out there for a whole afternoon. 'Yes,' he thought to himself, 'most odd ...'

Mrs Armstrong recovered from her supposed chill, and on the following Wednesday enjoyed a hearty lunch of boiled leg of mutton, potatoes and savoy cabbage, followed by junket with preserved gooseberries. Afterwards she was taken ill with vomiting, and Dr Hincks was called in. He noted a dark, almost coppery tint to her normally sallow skin, and sores around her lips. Vomiting continued, and she was stricken with diarrhoea and stomach pains. The doctor noted with alarm that her pulse rate had risen to 120. He was asked to attend her daily, and the Major also sought the doctor's permission for his wife to continue taking her favourite homoeopathic remedies, which he was in the habit of preparing for her himself. Curiously, the doctor made no objection, despite the fact that he was himself treating her with conventional medicines. He told the Major that his wife must have no solid food, only milk-puddings and the like.

Two days later Mrs Armstrong found that she could not move her arms or legs. Paralysis had set in, and Dr Hincks told the Major that he thought it unlikely that his wife would recover. The Major seemed to take the news very calmly.

Early on the morning of Tuesday, 22 February, Nurse Allen, the nurse who had tended the sick woman since 27 January, looked at her patient and immediately summoned the Major from the separate bedroom he had used since his wife's return from the hospital. It was 8 a.m. when Dr Hincks was summoned. There was little he could do for Mrs Armstrong; it was all too obvious that she was at the point of death. Even so, Major Armstrong asked the doctor to drop him off at his office on his way out. The doctor left him at 9 Broad Street, where the legal practice was situated, at 9 a.m. Fifteen minutes later Nurse Allen telephoned the Major to inform him that his wife had just died.

There was virtually no possible shorter note the bereaved husband could have made in his diary about his wife's death. Against the date he simply wrote, 'K. died'.

The household staff now prepared and laid out the body. After it had been placed in a coffin and a candle lighted at the head, Major Armstrong removed his dead wife's rings from her fingers, watched by the maid.

Dr Hincks was still puzzled as he wrote out the death certificate, in which he stated the cause of death as heart disease, nephritis and gastritis. He remained puzzled after he had written it, and he was puzzled for some time to come. He just could not reconcile the symptoms: darkened skin, mouth ulcers, rapid pulse rate, paralysis of the limbs, vomiting and diarrhoea. He had treated other patients with gastritis, and they had not presented all these symptoms. Nephritis per se did not produce them either. An autopsy is what he would have liked, but to ask for an autopsy was unthinkable, because it would doubtless have upset some small-town middle-class susceptibilities.

Three weeks after his wife was buried – noted in his diary by the succinct entry 'K's funeral 3 p.m., Cusop' – the Major was enjoying a month's holiday in Italy and Malta, and on his return he asked Marion Gale to marry him. This she declined to do. Still, the frustrated Major did not allow unrequited love to distract him from what was now going to be his main occupation – reviving his sadly-neglected legal practice. Into this work he threw himself with commendable zeal. After all, many bereaved men and women find a degree of consolation in applying themselves wholeheartedly to their work.

While Major Armstrong had been so occupied with domestic matters and had frequently been absent from the office where he was the only practising solicitor, it is hardly surprising that his erstwhile clients had transferred their allegiance to the only other solicitor in Hay-on-Wye, whose name was Oswald Martin. It was convenient, too, because Mr Martin's office was directly opposite Major Armstrong's office in Broad Street, so, when the latter was not to be found, all the client had to do was to cross the road and he or she would find a lawyer able and willing to deal with the matters concerned.

Major Armstrong, now that he was back in harness and looking into his affairs very carefully, was horrified to find that Mr Martin had creamed off a large percentage of his clients and had by now become a formidable rival. Clearly something must be done; Major Armstrong could not allow this state of affairs to continue. After all, it was his livelihood and that of his family that were at stake. Anyway, who was this upstart to challenge a long-established professional practice? The fellow was young – not yet thirty – and had served throughout the entire war as a private without even making NCO status. Major Armstrong decided on a few scare tactics. He laced a box of Fuller's chocolates with an irritant chemical and sent it to Mr Martin anonymously.

Mr Martin and his wife fortunately had no fondness for chocolates, so they put them on one side for some occasion when they had guests. They had no idea who had sent them, nor did they try to discover the sender's identity thinking that no doubt it was one of their clients, satisfied with the outcome of some legal deal.

On 8 October the Martins gave a dinner party for the young solicitor's two brothers and their wives, who were in Hay-on-Wye on a visit. They offered the box of chocolates round after the dinner with the coffee. Only Dorothy, the wife of Gilbert Martin, ate any of the chocolates. It seemed that none of the other guests liked chocolates either. Later that night Dorothy Martin was taken ill, seized with vomiting and stomach cramps. She attributed this to the shrimp cocktail, thinking that perhaps she must be allergic to seafood, which she did not normally eat.

At about this time a local Inland Revenue official was taken ill after dining at Mayfield, and a Mr Davies, an estate agent, likewise. Major Armstrong thought that perhaps these trial runs served no useful purpose: it was Martin he had a real grudge against. More decisive action was called for.

Quite apart from the poaching of some of his best clients, the young solicitor was acting for the purchaser of a large estate, in which Major Armstrong was acting for the vendor. Contracts had been exchanged, the deposit paid, but the completion of the sale was more than a year overdue. On 20 October 1921 Mr Martin gave Major Armstrong strong written notice of his client's desire to rescind the contract and demanded the return of his deposit with interest, costs and expenses incurred. This annoyed the Major intensely. However, he decided that an apparent conciliatory attitude might be the wisest course to adopt and, accordingly, he invited his rival to tea at Mayfield on Wednesday, 26 October.

Mr Martin, arriving at about 5.15 p.m., was met by Major Armstrong in the drive as he was parking his car. First the Major showed his visitor round the garden, and they then went into the house. In the drawing-room the maid had laid out a small tea-table near the window with various items, including a three-tier cake stand containing buttered scones. The maid entered with the silver teapot and a jug of hot water.

Major Armstrong poured out a cup of tea and handed it

to his guest. 'Please help yourself to milk and sugar,' he said. 'I'm not sure how much you like.' Then the Major took a scone from the top tier of the cake stand and handed it to Mr Martin. 'Excuse fingers,' he said. Mr Martin must have been struck by this gesture, so uncharacteristic of an educated man, but he said nothing.

It is not known what business arrangements the two rivals came to at this meeting, nor whether some kind of truce in the estate deal was arrived at. What is known is that Mr Martin, after supper with his wife that night, suddenly felt horribly nauseous and dashed up the stairs to the bathroom to be sick. He continued to vomit throughout the night, and was so ill that he had to stay in bed for five days. A doctor was called; none other than Dr Hincks. And if the doctor had been puzzled by Mrs Armstrong's symptoms, he was even more so by those presented by Mr Martin. No ordinary food, such as buttered scones or the light supper he had eaten, could cause symptoms of such severity.

Fortunately, however, the doctor had a visitor who was able to provide a possible solution to the enigma. The visitor was his father-in-law, Hay-on-Wye's chief chemist, John Davies. The two had an earnest conversation, during which the chemist mentioned that Major Armstrong was a keen gardener and had purchased a substantial quantity of arsenic from him to kill weeds, 'and so early in the year, too.' The sudden sickness of Dorothy Martin then sprang to mind. It was decided that, as a precautionary measure, the few remaining chocolates in the box, which was still in the Martins' house, as well as a urine sample from the still unwell young solicitor, should be sent to the Clinical Research Association's laboratory in London. At the same time Dr Hincks summoned up his courage and addressed a letter outlining his suspicions to the Home Office. It might stir up a hornets' nest and bring down the wrath of the Hay-on-Wye upper middle-class on his head, but better that than a few upper middle-class citizens lying dead.

The laboratory found that several of the chocolates had been tampered with and contained arsenic in varying amounts, one as much as 2.12 of a grain. The urine sample contained 0.33 of a grain of arsenic. The Home Office, however, did not contact Dr Hincks until 9 December, when a representative of the Director of Public Prosecutions arranged a meeting with Dr Hincks in Hereford. A police investigation was inaugurated, but it was to be kept secret until such time as it was thought expedient to come into the open.

Major Armstrong was, of course, completely unaware of all these moves, and with the persistence born of desperation continued to bombard Mr Martin, after his recovery, with invitations to tea. The young lawyer found it difficult to stave off these invitations with increasingly lame excuses. 'I must have had twenty invitations to take tea at Mayfield,' he was later to say. It is hard to know how a man who had the intelligence to qualify as a solicitor did not realize that he could not but fail to draw attention to himself with this continual barrage of invitations.

In order to avoid passing Mayfield on his way home, Mr Martin began to take tea in his office. The Major soon got wind of this and began to do likewise. Since their offices were opposite one another on the same street, it became increasingly difficult for Mr Martin to cook up plausible excuses not to accept the invitations which now came his way by telephone to take tea with the Major in his office. On police instructions, he had to avoid giving the Major any cause for alarm when he politely declined the offer to 'nip across the road and discuss business over a cup of tea'.

Just before Christmas Major Armstrong sent a formal invitation to Mr and Mrs Martin to join him at dinner at Mayfield on 28 December. The hapless Martins declined the invitation with the excuse that they already had a prior engagement to dinner with in-laws, and braced themselves for what they were sure would be a further invitation for an alternative date. However, Inspector Crutchett of the Yard rescued them from their unenviable situation by calling on the Major in his office, accompanied by Superintendent Weaver, the Deputy Chief Constable of Herefordshire, and a sergeant named Sharp. It was 10 a.m. on the last day of the year.

Major Armstrong was arrested on a charge of attempting to murder Mr Martin, and his office was searched. Two ounces of arsenic were found in a drawer of his office desk, and a small packet of the poison was discovered in the pocket of the jacket he was wearing. The Major was taken to the police station and kept in custody there, to the stunned amazement of the court officials with whom he had so often worked. Their astonishment knew no bounds when they learned that their respected colleague was remanded to Worcester jail.

An exhumation order was obtained with all possible celerity, and on 2 January 1922 the body of Mrs Armstrong was exhumed in the snowbound churchyard at Cusop Dingle. The following day the body was in the pathology laboratory for forensic examination by Bernard Spilsbury, who had not yet received his knighthood and was just 'Doctor'. He found 3.5 grains of arsenic in the body, which was a mere remnant of the massive dose which had killed her. Even as the gravediggers toiled in the frozen ground, Major Armstrong was making his first court appearance in the Magistrates' Court of Hay-on-Wye where he had formerly been involved in the procedures of justice. His appearance on a charge of murder created a sensation, and on 19 January he was formally charged with the murder of his wife and sent for trial at Hereford Assizes.

As the trial opened on Monday, 3 April 1922, snow was falling, most unseasonably. The judge was Mr Justice Darling, then seventy-three; the Attorney-General, Sir Ernest Pollock, led for the prosecution, and Major Armstrong was defended by Sir Henry Curtis-Bennett, who suggested that Mrs Armstrong had committed suicide while of unsound mind. He was also at pains to point out that Major Armstrong had barely touched the money which his wife had left to him, £2278 or so, which was a tidy sum in 1922.

The Major, a lawyer himself, proved to be a confident witness on his own behalf, and he clearly anticipated an acquittal. But he had not reckoned with Mr Justice Darling's skill as a criminal trial judge. His incisive questions wore the accused man's patience and ingenuity to a shadow, and his five hours in the witness-box took their toll. He could give no satisfactory explanation for the presence of arsenic in his office desk drawer and even in his jacket pocket while he was in the office; after all, he could not put forward a claim to have needed them for his garden while he was at work.

Major Armstrong was found guilty of the murder of his wife after a ten-day trial, all the famed advocacy of Sir Henry Curtis-Bennett having failed to save him from the gallows. He appealed, but the appeal was dismissed, and he was hanged at Gloucester Prison on 31 May 1922.

The two offices in Hay-on-Wye, are no longer occupied by the two firms of solicitors. I often wonder whether any of the present occupiers ever talk about, or even remember, the drama that had been played out in their premises more than sixty years ago.

3
The Elusive Mr Ng

It all started as a run-of-the-mill shoplifting case. An assistant in a DIY store in San Francisco had spotted a man walking out with a carpentry vice which he had not paid for. The assistant called the security guard, who summoned the police. A deputy named Daniel Wright arrived just in time to see the suspect putting the vice into the trunk of a car, and started towards him at a smart trot. The suspect, seeing the officer, took to his heels and dodged around parked cars, easily outrunning the heavily-built deputy. The suspect, youthful and slenderly-built, soon vanished into the traffic and disappeared.

All the frustrated deputy could do was to examine the car and make a note of its licence number. As he approached the car he saw that the passenger seat was occupied by a middle-aged, balding, bearded man. Wright removed the vice from the trunk of the car, which was not locked.

'It's all a misunderstanding, Officer,' the bearded man said. 'Charlie thought I had already paid for it.'

'Charlie? Who's Charlie?'

'The Chinese guy you saw run off. I hired him to do some work for me. I don't know his other name.'

The deputy thought it odd that a man would employ anybody without knowing their last name, but said nothing. Casual labour seemed to be getting more casual all the time. 'What's in that tote bag in the trunk?' he said.

'How do I know? It's not mine. It must be Charlie's. Whatever it is, he couldn't have wanted it all that much if he left it in my car when he ran off.'

The officer opened the bag. It contained a .22 automatic pistol fitted with a silencer. Wright informed the man that it was illegal to own or have in one's possession a weapon fitted with a silencer.

'Well, you'd better tell Charlie that – if you can find him,' the man replied. 'It's certainly not mine.'

'Let me see your driving licence,' the officer continued. The man offered a Californian driving licence in the name of Robin Scott Stapley, with an address in San Francisco.

Wright informed the man that he would have to accompany him to police HQ while they ran a computer check on him and his car. He would then be charged with illegal possession of a weapon fitted with a silencer, and be released on bail.

At the police-station, Stapley was shown into an interview room and when seated at the table he asked for a glass of water. A deputy brought him water in a paper cup. Stapley took a small capsule from his pocket, popped it into his mouth and swallowed a gulp of water. Almost immediately he slumped forward unconscious face down on the bare wooden table. The officers called an ambulance, telling the paramedics that their suspect had suffered a heart attack while in custody.

It was not long before the doctors in the emergency room at the local hospital reported back that the man had not had a heart attack at all, but had taken poison. He was now on a life-support machine, but was already brain-dead and they did not think he was going to make it.

'Now why would the guy want to commit suicide just because we'd nabbed him on a weapons violation?' Inspector Thomas Eisenmann, who was assigned to the case, mused aloud to one of his colleagues. 'And who is that Chinese guy who did a runner? There must be more to this than meets the eye. Have you had that computer check through yet on this chap and his car?'

'It's just come through now,' the officer replied. 'It seems this guy is not Robin Scott Stapley at all. Stapley is only twenty-six – this guy must be forty-five if he's a day. Stapley's been missing for several months. And – guess what? Two months ago Stapley's pickup and camper trailer were involved in a collision, but he wasn't driving it at the time. The report says it wasn't being driven by Stapley but by a Chinese youth. When the insurance company checked, the youth couldn't be traced. He'd obviously given a false ID.'

'Sounds like it could be our Charlie,' commented Wright. 'This case is getting curiouser and curiouser by the minute.'

His colleague continued to read from the computer print-out. 'That's not all,' he said. 'When the car was checked out the technicians found two spent slugs, bullet holes and dried bloodstains on the seats, and it had false licence plates.'

'Whew!' breathed Eisenmann. 'Let's get to the bottom of this.' Further checks revealed that the car did not even belong to Stapley. It was registered to a thirty-nine-year-old San Francisco car dealer named Paul Cosner. Seven months before the accident involving the car, he had gone missing along with his car. His girlfriend had reported that he had told her shortly before this that he had sold his car to 'a weird-looking guy' who was going to pay cash on delivery for the vehicle.

Further checks of the car revealed several bills from utility companies stashed in the glove compartment. These were all made out to a Charles Gunnar, with a rural address near Wilseyville, in Calaveras County.

'Looks like we've got two missing persons and two stolen cars,' Eisenmann said thoughtfully. 'Not to mention the missing Chinaman – who may be the key to this whole puzzle.'

'Who is the guy in the hospital, then?' Wright asked. 'Could he be Charles Gunnar?'

'Haven't the foggiest,' Eisenmann said. 'They're running a fingerprint check on him right now. One thing I do know, and that is, he couldn't have just hired the Chinese youth to do odd jobs. There must be some other explanation.' He studied the reports carefully. 'Tell you what,' he said, 'I think you'd better nip up to see the sheriff in Calaveras County tomorrow morning. See if you can come up with anything.' He detailed two officers to make the trip.

The sixty-year-old Sheriff Claude Ballard had spent most of his life in law enforcement and twenty-five years in Calaveras County. He immediately recognized the name of Charles Gunnar. 'He's one of those survivalists – you know, all stocked up against the nuclear holocaust they imagine is coming. He moved into a three-acre ranch near Wilseyville and built an underground anti-nuclear fallout shelter. It's constructed of cinder blocks and built into the side of a hill, and covered with tons of dirt. It would take some bomb to bust open that lot.'

'Anything on a young Chinese, late teens, slender build, wears horn-rimmed spectacles?'

'Oh, that would be Charlie – Charles Ng. That's spelled N G, and you pronounce it "Ing". He didn't live at the ranch, but was seen to go there quite a lot. An associate of Gunnar – no doubt about it. The two of them were always advertising a strange assortment of goods, from furniture, fridges, television sets, car spares, tools, fluorescent tube lighting sets, to jewellery and good quality men's clothing – sheepskin jackets and the like. We think they were all stolen, but we've not been able to prove it. Advertised in the local papers. We couldn't connect the stuff to any local burglaries. A lot of the stuff was new.'

While the officers were in conference in the sheriff's office, a call came through from San Francisco. 'The guy in the hospital isn't Gunnar,' the report said. 'We've got a make from his fingerprints which are on file. Name's Leonard Lake.'

Back at headquarters, Eisenmann was frankly puzzled by the new twists of complexity the case was taking. 'Run a computer check on Lake,' he ordered.

Lake was a native of San Francisco and had served in Vietnam as an aviation technician. He had been discharged in 1971 with what were described by the military authorities as 'psychiatric problems'. After his discharge he returned to California and settled in Mendocino County. He became obsessed with a possible nuclear holocaust – which he said was inevitable – and went around most of the time dressed in camouflage army fatigues. He gathered around him a small coterie of like-minded individuals and formed a survivalist group.

In 1982 Lake was arrested on burglary charges and also with the possession of illegal automatic weapons and explosives. At the time of his arrest a Chinese youth, Charles Ng, had been with him. Ng was wanted on a federal warrant as a fugitive from a court-martial conviction. Lake jumped bail while awaiting trial and went into hiding at a relative's ranch in Calaveras County, using the name of Charles Gunnar. A check on Gunnar revealed that he had been a close friend of Lake, who was reported missing at about the same time that Lake fled Mendocino County.

A check run on Charles Ng revealed that he was the youngest son of a wealthy family in Hong Kong. Educated in an English boarding-school, he was there only a short time before he was expelled for thefts from his fellow pupils. He was then sent to San Francisco to live with relatives and attend high school. He was involved in a hit-and-run car offence and, to escape prosecution, he joined the Marines in 1979. An expert in martial arts, he styled himself a 'Ninja warrior'. When he made lance-corporal he was posted to Hawaii, where he, together with two other Marines, was charged with the theft of three grenade launchers, two machine-guns, seven pistols and a night-sighting scope valued at $11,400. Charles Ng admitted masterminding the robbery and was court-martialled, but while awaiting sentence he escaped from custody and made his way to California. When and how he made the acquaintance of Lake and became involved with his survivalist group could not be ascertained.

After his arrest with Lake he was handed over to the military authorities and sent to the federal prison at Fort Leavenworth in Kansas. When parole was granted he avoided being deported to Hong Kong by claiming that he had been born in California. He returned to San Francisco, where he rented an apartment and obtained a job as a warehouseman. He quickly renewed his association with Lake, then using the name of Charles Gunnar.

When Eisenmann had passed on all this information to Sheriff Ballard in Calaveras County, the latter wondered whether all this might have any bearing on what he described as 'some strange goings-on' in his area. A family named Bond – Lonnie, his wife Brenda and their young child – had been neighbours of Lake. Several months previously they had mysteriously disappeared. Their friends and relations had said that the family had never mentioned to them any intention of leaving, nor had they ever heard from them since. After they had seemingly vanished into thin air, Lake – calling himself Gunnar – offered the furniture from their house for sale, claiming that Lonnie Bond had given the items to him in settlement of an outstanding loan.

The sheriff's deputies had also been investigating another equally strange disappearance. A couple had been camping at Lake Schaad, about a mile from Lake's ranch. Other campers reported that the couple had mysteriously vanished after going for a walk in the nearby woods, leaving behind all their camping gear, cooking utensils and food. The sheriff's deputies had been unable to obtain identification for the couple, and did not know whether they had a car or had been backpacking. They checked missing person reports but had come up blank.

Sheriff Ballard now obtained a search warrant for the Lake ranch and he, with his deputies, accompanied by Eisenmann and a colleague, went out to the ranch, which was hidden from the road by thick woods. The drive was barred with a locked iron gate. They scrambled over the fence and as they approached the ranch-style farm house they spotted a pick-up truck parked nearby. It matched the description of the stolen pick-up in their computer print-out.

Although the house was locked, the officers effected an entry and in the main living-room they found videos, books and magazines on survivalist techniques and gun racks along the walls. The master bedroom had a large bed, above which were shackles and chains secured to eye bolts in the ceiling and along the walls. The fall-out bunker built into the hillside was behind the house.

The sheriff, along the route to the house, had spotted a trench which appeared to have been fairly recently dug from the road up to the house, as though to locate power lines underground. He considered it distinctly odd that anyone would want to route electricity cables or telephone wires underground in such an isolated rural location. 'Why would the guy want to put the lines underground out here?' he said. Then he turned to his two deputies and told them to get more men out to the location. 'Tell them to start digging,' he said. 'It's my hunch there's something more than just power lines buried down there.'

Meanwhile Sergeant Audrey Brunn, Eisenmann's

colleague from HQ, was examining the costly video equipment in the living-room. She remembered that a few months previously she had been assigned to investigate the disappearance in mysterious circumstances of a family from San Francisco, Harvey Dubs, his wife Deborah and their sixteen-month-old son. Like the Bond family, they had not notified anybody that they were leaving. Dubs had not informed his employer that he intended giving up his job, nor had he picked up the month's wages he had due to him.

Neighbours had reported that at about the time the Dubs family vanished they had seen a Chinese youth moving furniture out of their apartment. Officer Brunn had been unable to locate this man, but she had ascertained that Dubs had recently purchased some high-quality video equipment. She wondered whether there was any connection.

'There's only one way to find out,' Eisenmann said. 'Check the serial numbers with the ones you got from the store where Dubs bought the stuff.' She did – and they matched.

The deputies now moved out to the bunker. After they had broken in, thankful that there were no gun-toting survivalists in residence at the time to offer resistance, they noted the contents of the main room, which was filled with survival gear of every description from food and water to medical supplies and automatic rifles with boxes of ammunition. What looked like the door to a wall closet was merely a cover for a trapdoor which led down a few steps to another room below. In this room was a large bed; on one wall was a forest-scene mural, and on another wall were dozens of photographs of young women and girls in varying degrees of nudity and provocative poses. On the ceiling were a number of brownish stains that looked like old blood splashes.

'I'll be goddamned!' exploded the sheriff. 'What do you make of it?' He addressed all and sundry. No one was able to give him an answer.

There was a shout from outside. It was one of the diggers. 'We've found something in that trench,' he said. 'I'm pretty damn sure they are human bones. And some teeth. And we've found more scattered over the ground on the hillside. And hidden in the woods there are two fifty-gallon drums and a metal bin. Looks like they've been used to cremate bodies.' The deputy reporting in with the discovery looked distinctly ashen-faced.

Ballard and Eisenmann went out to the site where the bones had been found. 'Don't touch anything or attempt to lift them out until the technicians get here,' they said. 'We'll send for them now and leave you to guard the remains.'

A screech of tyres signalled the arrival of three cars full of police technicians and detectives. Detective Steve Matthews examined the remains. 'They're human, all right,' he confirmed. 'Look at those teeth.' The officers, looking where he pointed, saw that the teeth were those of a young child.

Another digger joined the group. 'We've found two more bodies,' he said. 'They're badly decomposed, so it's impossible for us to say if they are the bodies of men or women, but they're adults, from the size. The Doc will be able to tell us more after the autopsy.'

A call was put through to Eisenmann's superior at HQ, and Ballard put in a call to the County Coroner. Both arrived shortly, together with the police doctor. Eisenmann asked about Lake. 'Any news from the hospital?'

'He's unplugged,' was the reply. 'Irreversibly clinically dead.'

'Any more news on the elusive Mr Ng?'

'We checked out his apartment. Apparently he made straight there after Officer Wright picked up Lake, grabbed some gear and split. He hasn't been seen since. We've put out an alert for him.'

The search of the house was still continuing. Two handwritten diaries, totalling more than 500 pages, were found in a desk drawer. They constituted a daily journal of Lake's activities. Hardened detectives gasped in horror at the detailed descriptions of vicious beatings of victims, perverted sex, torture, murder and the cremation of bodies. 'No wonder the guy committed suicide,' Eisenmann commented.

In the diaries, Lake had referred to videotapes he had made of his activities. A search was instituted for these, and it was not long before they came to light. The diary entries had not just been the fantasies of a disordered mind – the atrocities were recorded on tape for anyone to see.

A young woman, shackled nude to a chair, was shown being threatened by Lake, who said, 'I will put a bullet in your head if you do not satisfy me.' The man wore a black mask which effectively disguised his face, but the voice was unmistakably Lake's.

Another tape showed a young woman, bound to the same chair, a man answering the description of Charles Ng standing beside her brandishing a hunting-knife. The young woman was pleading to know what the men had done with her baby. The man resembling Ng then slashed off her clothes with the knife as she continued to beg for the life of her child.

Several of the tapes showed young women being forced at knifepoint or at gunpoint to commit sexual acts. Others showed young women shackled in chains and scarred from vicious beatings.

By the following morning twenty top homicide detectives had arrived from San Francisco HQ, and Sheriff Ballard assigned more than half of his forty-strong force to the case. The State Department of Justice also sent in twelve of their top agents and a number of technicians in mobile crime labs.

In the state capital there was a new development in the hunt for Charles Ng. Michael Sean Carroll, a twenty-three-year-old marine who had known Ng, and his eighteen-year-old girlfriend Kathleen Allen, had been reported missing after they had left with Ng to visit Lake's ranch. Later the girlfriend was identified on one of the videotapes as one of the victims bound to a chair and threatened by Ng with a knife.

Technicians tediously collected the charred bones that had been scattered on the hillside. Most were in small fragments, very few being more than three inches or so in length. Forty-five pounds of the remains were collected, including sets of teeth from child victims. A search in the vicinity of the bunker turned up a bloodstained power saw which had apparently been used to dismember the bodies prior to cremation in the drums found on the property. Four more bodies were disinterred from the trench where the deputies had steadily continued digging.

State Attorney John van der Kamp, who had been placed in overall charge of the investigation, realized that identification of the young women victims would be impossible without the release of head shots enlarged from the photographs which had been on the wall at the ranch. He asked that anyone who might know them should report to the police immediately in an effort to determine whether they were still missing, or known to be alive.

A new lead came in on Charles Ng. A gun dealer in San Francisco reported that he had received a call from Ng in Chicago asking him to return an automatic pistol he had left with him for repair. Ng wanted him to send it to him in the name of 'Mike Kimoto' c/o General Delivery at a named post office. The gunsmith replied that it was against federal law to ship handguns across state lines, but if he wanted the gun it could be shipped to a dealer in Chicago and picked up there. Ng became angry and told the dealer to forget it, adding that if he reported the call to the police Ng would come and kill him. The public-spirited gunsmith ignored the threat and notified the police that the much wanted and elusive Mr Ng was in Chicago.

A check on 'Mike Kimoto' revealed that a person using that name, who appeared to be Chinese rather than Japanese as the name would imply, had purchased an airline ticket on the evening of the day when Ng had managed to elude Officer Daniel Wright outside the DIY shop. 'Kimoto' was traced to the Chateau Hotel in Chicago, but by the time police arrived Ng had checked out. He was still one step ahead …

Investigators realized that Ng could well be heading for Toronto, Canada, where there is a large Chinese population and where he might have relatives or could lose himself in the community. The Canadian authorities were asked to keep a sharp lookout and were furnished with Ng's description.

Meanwhile the search at the ranch continued. Police with dogs located a grave in the woods about a mile from the house. A man and a woman had been shot with a small-calibre weapon and buried in their own sleeping-bags. They were thought to be the campers reported missing from Lake Schaad.

At a Press conference some weeks later, the State

Attorney informed the reporters that nine victims had been positively identified, and that there were several others as yet unidentified owing to the advanced state of decomposition of the bodies or because they had been reduced to fragmented bones. The videotapes, however, placed Kathleen Allen at the ranch, and it would seem that Michael Carroll, her boyfriend, had been killed also. Deborah Dubs and Brenda Bond were both identified from the tapes with a clear indication that they had been killed and that their husbands and children had suffered the same fate. 'We have definitely established that at least twenty-five persons known to Ng and Lake have been reported missing,' John van der Kamp continued. 'We do not know how many more there may be, and it is likely that we may never be able to make a positive identification on all the victims because they were cremated and their bones are unidentifiable.'

Van der Kamp said that Ng's participation in at least some of the murders was substantiated both in Lake's diaries and the videotapes. And he added that two men who had worked with Ng had also been reported missing, although they did not figure either in the diaries or the tapes. 'Unless we can locate Ng and get him to talk, we shall probably never know the half of what went on out there,' he concluded.

The police theory that Ng would make for Canada paid off. He was sighted in Sudbury, west of Toronto, apparently heading for the west coast. If he could reach Vancouver, British Columbia, it was feared he could take ship for Hong Kong and escape from their jurisdiction altogether.

On the afternoon of Saturday, 6 July, just over a month since Ng had fled from the DIY store in San Francisco, a security guard in the grocery section of Hudson's Bay Department Store in Calgary, Alberta, spotted a Chinese youth slipping a packet of cookies under the jacket he was wearing. The guard, John Doyle, approached the youth. 'Look here, young fellow! In this store we expect you to pay for what you take.'

The youth's reaction was quite unexpected. He whipped a .22 automatic pistol from the belt of his trousers. As he did so the cookies, along with a can of beans, a

plastic-wrapped package of cooked herring and a length
of rope cascaded from inside his jacket to the floor. The
unarmed guard made a grab for the pistol. Two shots were
fired; one went wide, the other slug clipped the top of one
of Doyle's fingers. The sound of the shots alerted other
security staff as the youth fled through the store. A flying
tackle brought him to the ground and the gun flew from
his hand. Police were called and quickly handcuffed him.
The long-sought fugitive was captured at last. Among
papers in various names found in his possession, one was
a driving licence in the name of Charles Ng.

Doyle was rushed to hospital, where his wound was
found to be only superficial, and he was soon able to
return to his duties, where he found he had become a hero
overnight. Meanwhile the Canadian authorities were
jubilant at being able to inform the FBI that Ng was, at
long last, in custody. They, in turn, informed the
investigators in San Francisco and Calaveras County.
Immediately six representatives of the San Francisco
police, the Calaveras County Sheriff's office and the State
Department of Justice left for Calgary to question the
suspect. They were able to spend a total of five hours with
Ng, which they said had been very productive. Thereafter
court-appointed attorneys advised Ng to make no further
statements to law enforcement officers.

One of the San Francisco police officers who
interrogated Ng, Inspector George Kowalski, said that Ng
placed all the blame for the sexual torture of the women,
the murders, the dismemberment, cremation and burial of
the victims' bodies upon Lake. 'We expected that,'
Kowalski was reported as saying, 'but we did get enough
out of him to enable us to start putting a case together.'

State Attorney van der Kamp petitioned to have Ng
extradited to California. Owing to certain legal technicalities this was to prove difficult. Ng's attorneys stated that
they would strenuously resist extradition and they would
demand that if their client were extradited they would
demand a pledge from the Californian authorities that he
could not be charged with a capital crime that carried the
death penalty.

An option open in Canada would be to have Ng
deported as an undesirable alien, in which event Ng could

be sent to Hong Kong as a British subject, and it would be impossible to bring him to the United States from there to face trial.

Ng was arraigned before Judge Hubert Oliver in Calgary at a preliminary hearing on charges of attempted murder, unlawful use of a firearm, wounding the security guard and theft. The judge ordered that Ng be held without bail pending a forthcoming trial on these charges.

John van der Kamp tried not to be too despondent at the chances of getting Ng back to the United States. 'It may take months, even years,' he told reporters, 'but we're going to keep on trying until we do.'

Meanwhile Sheriff Ballard and the other investigators were still searching Lake's ranch and the surrounding area for more evidence – even for more bodies. 'It will probably take us five years or more to wrap this case up,' Ballard was quoted as saying. 'And even if we do manage to get Ng back to California to stand trial, he may refuse to talk, so we may never know the precise body count.'

Three of those five years have passed already. Ballard and his deputies are still looking, and Ng, in Canada, has not talked.

4
Murder on the Crumbles

There are a good many options open to a married man who finds a mistress becoming an importunate nuisance and wishes to be rid of her. One of these options is murder. And when the man invites the mistress to spend a weekend with him at the seaside and takes the precaution of buying a ten-inch cook's knife and a meat-saw beforehand to take with him to the romantic rendezvous, there you have as neat a proof of premeditated murder as any prosecutor could ever wish for.

Emily Beilby Kaye was no teenage daydreamer with her head in the clouds. Dreams she certainly had, but they were the more mature dreams of a woman of thirty-eight who had saved a modest nest-egg and knew where she was going. That is, until she was literally stopped dead in her tracks by her knife-wielding, saw-toting fiancé.

What Emily had in mind was to find a personable businessman with a steady job who, like herself, thought that there would be better employment prospects in one or other of the far-flung outposts of the Empire where, in those days, British working people were not only welcome but were in great demand and well-paid. Her idea was to marry such a man and emigrate with him to a new and better life. At thirty-eight she realized that she did not have so much time for a leisurely look around as a younger woman would. So, if she did not want to be 'left on the shelf', she had better get weaving. Unfortunately the tapestry she wove would eventually enmesh her in the toils of death.

Emily was working, at the time this story unfolds, as a secretary to one of the partners in a firm of chartered accountants, Messrs Robertson, Hill and Company, who

had offices in Copthall Avenue in the City of London. She
had managed to save £600 – a tidy sum in those days –
from her salary of £17 6s. 8d. per month, and had invested
these savings in stocks and shares. With her feet firmly on
the ground she had not gambled in speculative issues but
chose gilt-edged securities, government stocks and bonds
and similar 'safe' investments.

One way in which she was able to economize was to live
at a hostel for working women – rather like a YWCA in
type – called the Green Cross Club in Guildford Street, off
Russell Square, where she shared a room with another
middle-aged spinster named Edith Warren. The two
became firm friends and corresponded whenever one or
other of them went on holiday, although they did not,
apparently, spend any holidays together.

One day a good-looking Irishman with twinkling eyes
and a ready smile came into the office in his capacity as
sales manager of an office supply firm. Emily Kaye was
immediately drawn to him – a fatal attraction, as it turned
out. He was thirty-four, 5ft. 10ins. tall, and had thick
brown wavy hair; he was a good talker and a good
listener. One of the things he did *not* talk about, though,
was the fact that he had done time in prison for forgery
and embezzlement, passing dud cheques and robbery
with violence. After all, it would spoil his Irish blarney to
mention anything like that. This girl certainly seemed to
take to him; he would be very foolish to say anything that
could ruin his chances with her. Nor did he tell her that he
was married with a family in Richmond or that he was an
avid pursuer of women.

His constant picking up of girls had been the cause of
his losing more than one job prior to the one he now had.
It even interfered with his burglaries. At one house he had
knocked the maid out with a hammer, while afterwards he
stayed to bring her round with kisses and caresses,
accompanied by reassuring words of comfort and
apology. Conveniently, he was still there when the police
came to arrest him, without so much as a silver spoon out
of place.

The friendship between Emily Kaye and Patrick Herbert
Mahon, her new admirer whom she knew as simply 'Pat',
deepened, and Emily was soon besotted. She considered

him a little slow in regard to professing his love for her,
and frequently took the initiative in telephoning him at
work, inviting him to join her on outings and so on. This
caused him to say later that he considered her to be 'a
woman of the world'.

Emily lost her job with the firm of chartered accountants
on 21 October 1923; the record does not give a reason.
However, with her qualifications, she found no difficulty
in obtaining a new position almost immediately afterwards, as a shorthand-typist and bookkeeper with the
firm of Lewis, Schaverien and Company, the financiers, in
Old Bond Street. Her new salary was an improvement on
her previous remuneration.

In February 1924 she began to sell her stocks and shares
and to realize her other savings, opening an account with
the Midland Bank in Coleman Street, into which she put
all her assets. On 16 February she cashed a cheque for
£404, the bank giving her £400 in £100 bills and four 'ones'.
It was later found that she had given the £400 to Pat as her
half share in their proposed trip to South Africa to set up
home together there, as Pat had led her to believe that
they would do.

In March she fell ill with influenza, and afterwards went
to Bournemouth for a week's holiday to recuperate. After
the holiday she went to Southampton where Pat joined
her. He took her to a jeweller's named Cranbrook's, in the
High Street, where he bought a diamond-and-sapphire
cluster engagement ring for her. That night they
celebrated their engagement by sharing a double room at
the South-Western Hotel. When signing the register he
gave his real name of Patrick H. Mahon of Richmond.

On Emily's return to London she showed her
engagement ring to her friends, including Edith Warren at
the Green Cross Club. She was so excited that she even
rushed into the club secretary's room without knocking in
order to show her the ring. 'We've booked our passage!'
she cried. 'Just think! A new life in South Africa! Pat's
getting a new job lined up there right now!' Emily wrote in
similar vein to her married sister, Mrs Elizabeth Harrison,
who lived in Cheshire, on 5 April.

On that same day Patrick Mahon was in Langney, near
Pevensey Bay in Sussex, inspecting a bungalow which had

been advertised to let in *Dalton's Weekly*. Calling himself 'Waller' he met the letting agent there and agreed to rent it at three-and-a-half guineas a week from 11 April to 6 June. Known locally as 'The Officer's House', the bungalow was one of a small row of whitewashed houses once occupied by the coastguards, standing on a lonely stretch of shingle known as 'The Crumbles'.

Mahon arranged to meet Emily in Eastbourne on Saturday 12 April. He told her to bring with her the documents she would require for the wedding trip to South Africa – passport, birth certificate and so on. Full of joy, she could not wait until the Saturday to leave London, although she knew that Pat would not be able to join her until the 12th. On Monday 7 April she left her employers and took her leave of her friends as she moved out of the Green Cross Club. She gave a poste restante address to her friend Edith Warren. In Eastbourne she took a room at the Kenilworth Court Hotel and spent the rest of the week buying a trousseau and a smart going-away outfit.

On the 12th, wearing a smart grey costume with matching suede shoes and hat and a three-quarter-length fur coat, she checked out of the hotel. She said she would be sending a cab to pick up her luggage later, and gave the receptionist the poste restante address for the forwarding of mail. She met Mahon off the 4.49 p.m. train by prior arrangement. They took a cab, picked up her luggage from the hotel and drove out to the bungalow on the Crumbles.

Earlier that same day Mahon had been in Victoria Street, London, where he visited the Staines Kitchen Equipment Company's retail outlet there and purchased the ten-inch cook's knife and meat-saw. By what must surely be one of the strangest of coincidences, whom should he meet soon after coming out of the store with his deadly purchases? None other than Mr Muir, the estate agent who had met him at the bungalow and handed him the keys after the rental agreement had been signed and the rent paid!

Emily Beilby Kaye met her death that weekend. No one knows the exact time, but it is known that she was still alive on the Sunday, 13 April, because a butcher who called that morning to deliver some meat saw her, and later that same day Emily called at one of the neighbouring bungalows to borrow some milk. It seemed that she spent some of that day writing letters to her sister and her friends, in which she asked them to send mail to her c/o the Standard Bank in Cape Town, and promised to write more fully after her arrival in South Africa. These letters, although dated 14 April, were posted by Mahon on the 13th, so it would seem that she wrote them on the Sunday but put the wrong date on them.

One of her friends who was the recipient of one of these letters later said: 'When she introduced me to Pat, I thought there was something about him I could not quite put my finger on. He did not seem quite right somehow. I often wondered whether she was doing the right thing. And then emigrating like that at such short notice. Now if it had been me, I would have wanted several months to prepare for a trip like that. Still, I suppose she was old enough to know what she was doing.'

She certainly thought she did. After all, there was no possible way she could have known that her personable fiancé had purchased a butcher's knife and saw with her in mind.

It would appear that on the Sunday night Patrick Mahon and Emily Kaye had a violent quarrel. It seemed that, being compelled to admit to her that he was a married man and therefore could not marry her, and that he could not take her to South Africa to start a new life, she quite naturally became extremely upset. After all, she had given up her job, her home and her friends and thrown in her lot with this man she loved, for better or for worse. Now, at this late stage, he was telling her that it had all been for naught. He had nothing to offer her. She was also two months pregnant (this was confirmed later by Sir Bernard Spilsbury at the autopsy). In his confession Mahon denied that he knew she was pregnant and thought that it was a ploy to induce him to marry her.

Although Mahon was later to confess to the killing, he insisted to the last that it had been an accident. He averred that Emily had attacked him by throwing the chopper he had been using to prepare wood and coal for the fire at him. He said that she aimed at his head but missed, the chopper narrowly avoiding hitting him on the shoulder and hitting the door-frame instead. He went on to say that she had then 'leapt across the room clawing at his face.' It

should here be noted that there were no marks of damage
to the door, nor scratches on the accused's face, to
substantiate these claims, and those of her friends who
were called as witnesses at the trial all stated that 'Emily
was not the kind of person to lose her temper easily, never
mind attack somebody.'

Mahon then alleged that during this struggle Emily had
slipped (he admitted that in the struggle he could have
pushed her) and she fell and hit her head on the
coal-scuttle. This blow, he said, killed her. Sir Bernard
Spilsbury thought this extremely unlikely, since the
coal-scuttle, which was put into evidence in court at the
trial, was not a heavy iron, brass or copper scuttle but of
light and flimsy tin construction which could not have
caused an injury capable of killing a grown woman. Miss
Kaye, he pointed out, was tall, athletic in build and
weighed eleven stone, yet he could find no dent or other
mark of damage to the scuttle. Had someone that size
fallen head first on to it, it would have buckled under the
impact.

The discredited Mahon continued to stick to his story.
He continued by stating that after dashing cold water into
her face to try to revive her (this *after* stating that he knew
she was dead!) he left her body lying where it had fallen
and went out into the garden in a daze, from where he
went for a long walk along the beach trying to decide what
to do. He said that he returned to the house at dawn and
when he saw the body still lying there the enormity of
what he had done began to sink in. He dragged the body
into one of the bedrooms and covered it with her fur coat.
He then went to London, where he had an appointment to
meet another girl, Ethel Duncan, aged thirty-two and
unmarried, from Isleworth, whom he had met some time
previously. He invited her to spend the Easter weekend
with him at the bungalow. 'If I had not had her with me,'
he later told police, 'I should have gone stark raving mad. I
just had to keep my mind off ... it was ghastly.'

He now had a few days to dispose of the body before his
new girlfriend arrived. First he cut off the legs and the
head, emptied the victim's luggage trunk of her
belongings and put them into the wardrobe and drawers
in the room, and packed her torso into the improvised

coffin. He then locked the room and hid the key. After his guest, who had slept in the room next to that containing the trunk and leather bag containing the head and legs wrapped in newspaper, had returned to London on Easter Monday, he then set about destroying the evidence. He built a big fire in the grate and burned the legs and head. He told his counsel that when he put the head on the blazing fire the eyes opened. There was a storm raging at the time and there was a loud thunderclap just as this happened, followed by a flash of lightning, and he fled from the house in terror.

When he had calmed himself somewhat, he returned to the house and continued disposing of various other portions of the body. In his statement to the police he described his procedure thus: 'I had to cut up the trunk [of the body]. I also cut off the arms. I burned portions of them. I then had to think of some other method of disposing of the portions. I boiled some portions in a large cooking-pot. I cut up others into small pieces, and packed them in a brown bag. I threw some of them out of the train while travelling between Waterloo and Richmond ... I had intended to go home on Sunday night but as I could not dispose of all the portions between Waterloo and Richmond I went on to Reading and stayed at the Station Hotel in the name of Rees.' That was on the night of 27 April, arriving at about 7 p.m. The next morning he went to London, where he left the brown bag in the left-luggage deposit at Waterloo.

During all these comings and goings, the long-suffering wife of the Crumbles killer was becoming more and more suspicious. His job as a travelling sales manager certainly could be expected to involve him in frequent absences from home, but working over Easter? That was more than even a credulous wife could swallow. And Jessie Mahon was not credulous: she had long experience of her husband's constant philandering and the piecrust-thin excuses he made to cover them. She had to give her husband's coat to the cleaners and set about emptying the pockets: recently she had read in the newspaper of someone who had absent-mindedly handed the same cleaning firm a jacket with £40 in the pocket. The owner had had considerable difficulty in persuading his bank to replace the soggy bills. In her husband's coat pocket Jessie Mahon found the Waterloo left-luggage ticket.

On 30 April she took her suspicions to a friend and neighbour who had been a former policeman. She handed him the ticket and asked him to investigate. 'Pat couldn't have been working over Easter,' she pointed out. 'All the offices he has to visit would be closed for the holiday.'

The ex-detective presented the ticket at Waterloo and was handed the bag – a locked brown leather Gladstone bag. He prised the sides apart and was able to see what appeared to be bloodstained female underwear and also a knife. He returned the bag to the left-luggage deposit and gave the ticket back to Mrs Mahon, but did not tell her of his discovery, but he told Mrs Mahon not to give the coat to the cleaners and to put the ticket back in the pocket.

The next day the ex-detective communicated his suspicions to the Chief Constable of the CID, Frederick Wensley, who instructed Detective Chief Inspector Percy Savage to investigate. He, together with Detective Sergeant Frew, visited the Waterloo left-luggage deposit at about 7.15 p.m. He loosened the straps and peered into the bag through the sides. Police officers were then detailed to keep observation and ordered to detain and question anyone who came to collect the bag. They did not have long to wait.

At about 6.30 p.m. on the following day (2 May) Patrick Mahon arrived and paid 5d. to retrieve the bag. As he walked towards the York Road exit from the station he was stopped by Detective Sergeant Thompson. 'Is that your bag?' the officer asked. 'I believe so,' Mahon replied. 'Do you mind if I take a look inside?' the officer continued. 'I don't have the key with me,' said Mahon.

'In that case,' Thompson continued, 'you'll have to come with me to Kennington police station.' 'Rubbish!' retorted Mahon. Thompson soon disillusioned him, and took the suspect to the police station in his squad car, where he was searched. A bunch of keys was found in his possession. At about 8.30 p.m. Detective Chief Inspector Savage took Mahon, together with the as yet unopened bag, to Scotland Yard. Mahon was offered tea or coffee and sandwiches, but refused.

'Is that your bag?' Savage asked. 'Yes,' Mahon replied.

The bag was then opened with a key from the bunch Mahon had been carrying. A torn and bloodstained pair of bloomers, a scarf and two pieces of white silk material all similarly bloodstained, and a cook's knife were found, as well as a brown canvas tennis racket holder bearing the initials E.B.K. All the items reeked of disinfectant. 'How do you account for the blood on these things?' Mahon was asked. 'I carried home meat for the dogs,' he replied. 'That explanation won't do, you know,' Savage said. 'I'll have to detain you pending further inquiries.' Mahon shrugged. 'Suit yourself,' he said.

An hour later, Mahon said, 'I suppose you know everything. I'll tell you the truth.' He was given the customary caution, and made a detailed voluntary statement. This was taken down by Detective Inspector Hall; it took more than two hours. At about 1.30 a.m. Mahon collapsed and had to be revived with a glass of whisky before he could continue. He then completed the statement at about 2 a.m., read it through, made one or two minor corrections, initialled each page and signed it at the end.

Wensley was informed of Mahon's statement straightaway and in the early hours of Saturday, 3 May he and Savage drove to the bungalow, having first liaised with the East Sussex Constabulary. The Crumbles lay desolate in the early morning mist, and the officers were still not really sure of what they would find inside the house.

The bungalow looked inviting enough from the outside, with the rambler roses round the door and the cottage garden flowers outside growing right up to the whitewashed walls. But, once inside, the place stank. In a large locked trunk marked E.B.K., which the officers had to prise open with a crowbar, they were horrified to find the limbless torso of a woman, cut into four quarters. Nearby were a hatbox and a biscuit-tin; inside were the heart and other internal organs. A cooking-pot stood on the stove, in which boiled pieces of human flesh swam in a sea of water and fat. Charred bones lay in the grates of both the sitting-room and the dining-room, and more were found on an ash-dump in the back garden. Bloodstains covered the floor of the sitting-room and there were blood splashes on the door frame. The chopper referred to by Mahon was found hidden under coal in the coal-hole. A saw was found in the fireplace in the sitting-room and the coal-scuttle was found in the dining-room. The dead woman's personal belongings and clothes were found in the bedroom where the trunk had been stored. Some underclothes had been torn up to wrap some of the remains.

On Sunday morning Sir Bernard Spilsbury, the famous pathologist, arrived and had a table moved out into the back garden on which to lay out the remains and conduct his autopsy. Officers were detailed to dig the garden to find out whether Mahon had buried any of the remains there, but it appeared that he had not done so and digging was abandoned. The missing legs and head were never found, and Mahon's story of destroying them by fire was believed.

On Monday, 5 May 1924, Patrick Herbert Mahon was charged with the murder of Emily Beilby Kaye. He replied, 'It wasn't murder, as my statement clearly shows.' He was sent for trial at Sussex Assizes on Tuesday, 15 July 1924, before Mr Justice Avory. Sir Henry Curtis-Bennett, KC, led for the prosecution, and Mahon was defended by Mr J.D. Cassels, KC. Thousands of people thronged the precincts of the court, but there was room for only 200 inside. There was drama even before the trial commenced, for four jurors had to be replaced. Two fell ill, one fainted, and another asked to be excused.

Ethel Duncan was called as a witness, sobbing hysterically as she took the oath and when she was asked to identify the prisoner in the dock. Her voice was barely audible as she answered questions amid sobs.

Sir Bernard Spilsbury was the next witness to be called. The absence of the head prevented him from giving any concrete evidence of the cause of death such as strangulation or being hit on the head with the chopper, but he theorized that either of these methods could have been employed, or her throat could have been cut. He ruled out any possibility of accidental death caused by a fall on to the coal-scuttle. He also confirmed that the dead woman had been two months pregnant.

Sir Bernard pointed out that Mahon's alleged burning of the head was carried out in order to destroy completely any evidence there could have been of the method of killing used. Why he would burn the legs was less obvious; it seemed that they were perhaps too large or too awkward to make up into parcels, too big to fit into the bag, or too heavy to carry without dismemberment. And Mahon was no professional butcher or anatomist; the dismemberment of the corpse had been of the crudest kind. It may be that he was literally unable to saw through the legs at the correct joints. Connoisseur of women he professed to be, but all his knowledge was external and did not extend to their skeletal structure.

Late that same afternoon Mahon was called to give evidence on his own behalf, and during his account of how he dismembered the body a storm was brewing outside. At one point lightning flashed and there was a thunderclap which reverberated round the courtroom. Mahon blanched and trembled, and had great difficulty in controlling himself; no doubt he was forcibly reminded of the storm that occurred when he was burning the head of his unfortunate victim. Sweat poured from his forehead and he wiped his clammy hands on his silk handkerchief; he swayed and would have fallen if a policeman had not supported him. He was given a chair, and after a short interval to allow him to recover his composure, he was relentlessly cross-examined by Sir Henry Curtis-Bennett for three hours. Mahon wept as he answered Sir Henry's questions.

Saturday morning, 19 July, saw Mr Justice Avory giving his summing-up. Mahon sat huddled in his chair, seemingly indifferent; not once did he look up. The summing-up took an hour and a half, but the jury did not need so much time to deliberate on their verdict and return a finding of guilty of murder. Only then did Mahon suddenly leap to his feet, galvanized into activity by what he described as 'the bitterness, unfairness and bias' of the judge's summing-up when asked whether he wished to say anything before sentence was passed upon him.

Patrick Herbert Mahon was hanged at Wandsworth Prison on 9 September 1924.

The case created a precedent in medical jurisprudence. When Sir Bernard Spilsbury arrived at the bungalow on the Crumbles on 4 May to carry out the autopsy, he found

Detective Chief Inspector Savage handling the dreadful remains with his bare hands. What was left of the body was already far advanced into decomposition. 'Are there no rubber gloves?' Sir Bernard demanded. No gloves were available, and if anyone handling the material had a cut or sore on his hands he would have run a grave risk of infection. After the autopsy Sir Bernard held a conference at Scotland Yard with top-ranking police-officers and forensic experts, at which a scheme was put into operation that from then onwards a 'Murder Bag', containing all necessary requisites for the hygienic handling and transportation of any kind of scene-of-crime material to the forensic laboratory for examination, must be taken to the scene of any murder by the police-officers investigating the crime.

5

A Fire at the Metropole

Matricide is an ugly word. The crime itself is so odious, so repugnant, to the normal person that fortunately it is a very rare occurrence.

To murder one's own mother for her insurance is horrible enough, but when a son takes out insurance on her life only days before plotting to strangle her with his bare hands and cover up his crime with an act of arson, it is not only a murder most foul but also an example of a homicide requiring a great deal of premeditation and planning, especially as the policy would expire within twenty minutes of the death of the insured, which was certainly cutting things a bit close. Sidney Fox, however, had the diabolical cunning and the nerve to see it through to the end.

Sidney Fox was a ne'er-do-well who had never done a stroke of work in his life but lived by the misuse of his wits, aided and abetted by his equally feckless mother. For all her faults it cannot be denied that she was genuinely fond of Sidney, who was her youngest son, born in 1899. Her eldest son was killed in action in 1917, and she drew a war pension of ten shillings a week on his behalf. Two 'middle' sons had left home and were, apparently, gainfully employed and independent of the family. Mrs Rosaline Fox had by this time separated from her husband and this left her with just Sidney to keep her company as she never remarried or, as far as is known, even bothered to obtain a divorce. Sidney himself did not entertain thoughts of marriage, as he was homosexual. But Sidney certainly never led a gay life in the true meaning of the word: with his mother he trailed miserably from one rooming-house or cheap hotel to another, usually conning the management into allowing them credit and then when the inescapable end loomed, doing what is called a 'moonlight flit' and starting again elsewhere. The trail of unpaid debts they left behind them was prodigious: unpaid bills, dud cheques, and luggage left behind as a deposit when opened was found to contain only bundles of old newspapers. The old lady would be left in their rooms swigging herself into a stupor with cheap wine, while Sidney was out seeing whom he could con or swindle into parting with a few bob to keep them going for a bit longer. His only legitimate income was an eight-shillings-a-week war pension, derived from having been invalided out of the army soon after joining with an unspecified complaint. Whether this was genuine or faked is not known. But even in those days their combined income was insufficient to keep them even in the bare necessities of life. Eventually Mrs Fox, by the time she had reached the age of sixty-three, was reduced to wearing both her dresses at once (the only ones she had) because she no longer had a suitcase in which to keep any clothes. She did not even have a nightdress, but used to sleep in her vest. Sidney had only the suit he stood up in, which he managed to keep fairly presentable by assiduously brushing and cleaning it and hanging it up after each wearing.

In 1928 Sidney was sentenced to fifteen months' imprisonment for a jewellery theft. Not having Sidney around to defraud a few gullible tradesmen to augment their slender resources, Mrs Fox went to the workhouse. Among other ailments associated with the elderly, she suffered from Parkinson's disease, and while there she spent her time in the infirmary, where it is doubtful that she would have enjoyed her customary wine-bibbing sessions. In March 1929 Sidney was released, collected his mother from the workhouse and, together once more, they resumed their life of fraud. But the sands of time were running out for Sidney Fox …

On 21 April Sidney induced his mother to make a will, leaving all she had (which was not much) to her son. He had managed to discover a tiny insurance policy she had taken out on her life some twenty years previously. He paid up the arrears – no doubt at the expense of some honest but unsuspecting citizen. It is possible that the existence of this policy put the idea into Sidney's head of taking out further and more substantial policies, and it is known that the first of a series of accident policies on his mother's life was taken out on 30 April 1929. Two further policies, one for £1,000 and another for £2,000, were taken out subsequently. In order to save on premiums, Sidney took all these policies out for six-month periods with an option to renew.

The next six months saw this unscrupulous pair still on the circuit between hotels and boarding-houses, existing on credit, mainly by cashing cheques from stolen chequebooks. Sometimes, in desperation, they pawned their watches and even their spare clothes. From Canterbury and Folkestone (they had a predilection for the South-East) they arrived in Margate, where they took lodgings at the Metropole Hotel. This consisted of two adjoining rooms with a communicating door. When they arrived, on 16 October, they had only a few shillings between them, and all their worldly goods were contained in a small brown paper parcel. A suitcase was now an unattainable luxury. But the enterprising Sidney was soon going to change all that. Or so he thought ...

On 22 October Sidney announced to his mother that he had to go to London on business. He would take only a day trip, he assured her, and they would dine in the evening with a bottle of port which he would bring her. The fare and the port were paid for by a loan from a friend, and the business was to visit two of the insurance companies to extend until midnight on the following day the cover on their policies for £1,000 and £2,000 respectively. Knowing full well what he intended to do, Sidney showed his characteristic meanness by paying the premium for only one day's additional cover in each case. It seems incredible, however, that he should have left it right until the day the policies expired before renewing the cover, and it is certainly strange that the insurance companies did not query a one-day extension. Renewal for a further six months would have been a more normal procedure.

The wining and dining took place, not on Sidney's return from his trip, which he had timed too late at night to make feasible, but on the following night, 23 October.

The old lady seemed very happy in her port-induced stupor, and was helped to her favourite armchair after dinner by the ever-solicitous Sidney, who turned on the gas fire beside the armchair. He also left the newspaper on a table nearby.

At twenty minutes to midnight there was a fire alarm at the Metropole. The manager was called, and was just in time to see Mrs Fox, clad only in a vest, being dragged from her room, which was full of dense smoke, into the corridor. The manager dashed into the room with a towel over his face and managed to kick a badly-burned and still smouldering armchair into the corridor. The fire seemed to be confined to Mrs Fox's room. Sidney seemed remarkably calm, and it was he who had called the reception desk on the intercom to summon aid. The police were called in by the manager together with two doctors, who pronounced Mrs Fox dead. Both gave the cause of death as shock and suffocation. A death certificate was signed, and an inquest called for the next day, at which a verdict of death by misadventure was returned.

Sidney Fox did not waste time. Never a man to let the grass grow under his feet, he hastened immediately to a local solicitor, from whom he borrowed £40 on the strength of the insurance policies to pay for his mother's funeral on 29 October in the Norfolk village where she had been born. He left the Metropole Hotel without paying his bill, and on the morning of 29 October he was in Norwich discussing his insurance claims while his mother still lay in her coffin in the parish church prior to the funeral in the afternoon. After the funeral, which Sidney duly attended, he hastened back to Norwich to complete the negotiations for his claims, and in the evening registered at a small hotel, where he would, albeit unknowingly, spend the last few days of freedom he was to enjoy.

The manager of the Metropole Hotel, Margate, was an astute businessman who quickly realized that Sidney Fox was not only a scoundrel of the first water but that there was more behind the fire in his mother's room than met the eye. He decided to confide his suspicions to the police. After a bit of ferreting around, the local lawmen soon discovered that Sidney Fox was an undischarged bankrupt and as such had unlawfully obtained credit. On this charge he was arrested on 2 November. It was nominally a holding charge, because suspicions of a far more serious nature were accumulating. Within a week Scotland Yard had been called in, and Chief Inspector Hambrook, the famed 'Hambrook of the Yard', was on his way to the peaceful Norfolk country churchyard, accompanied by Sir Bernard Spilsbury, the great pathologist, whose name in forensic medicine was already legend.

The coffin had been sealed with putty, and because of this the putrefactive changes in the body were as yet minimal owing to the exclusion of air. Spilsbury's task at the post-mortem table was therefore a great deal less unpleasant than it had been when he had examined the remains of Emily Kaye. In conducting an autopsy Spilsbury was, of course, in a much better position to ascertain the precise cause of death than the two doctors who had been called in at the hotel, and it did not take long for him to find that the dead woman had not died of suffocation at all. In a case of death from suffocation by inhaling smoke, soot is found in the lungs and carbon monoxide in the blood. A minimum of forty-five per cent carbon monoxide in the blood would be required to cause death, and the amount usually found in such cases is nearer seventy per cent. Spilsbury found not a trace of carbon monoxide in the deceased's blood, nor did he find any soot in the lungs. Mrs Fox had been dead *before* the fire had started.

This is where many a murderer comes a cropper. Smoke, or water (as in the case of supposed drowning), cannot be inhaled: a dead body cannot inhale anything! Thus the pathologist can immediately tell whether death was caused by the effects of fire or water, or not, and if not then he must look for another cause.

Again Spilsbury did not have to look very long when examining the well-preserved body, having ruled out the fire as the cause of death. In the soft tissues between the larynx and the oesophagus he found a bruise the size of a half-crown. Its appearance and position led Spilsbury to the inevitable conclusion that Mrs Fox had died from manual strangulation.

Sidney Fox was charged with the murder of his mother and sent for trial at Sussex Assizes, held in the County Hall at Lewes. In many respects the trial bore similarities to that of Patrick Mahon for the murder of Emily Kaye: it was held at the same venue, the prosecution was led by Sir Henry Curtis-Bennett (with the Attorney-General, Sir William Jowitt), the accused was defended by Mr J.D. Cassels, and Sir Bernard Spilsbury gave evidence for the prosecution. Only the judge was different; this time it was Mr Justice Rowlatt. The trial opened on 12 March 1930.

The evidence of the fire at the Metropole Hotel was in itself very damaging to the accused. Although the armchair and the strip of carpet underneath the chair had been very badly burned, there was an unburned strip of carpet between the chair and the gas fire. How could a fire originating as alleged in the gas fire spread to the chair without having burned the carpet between it and the chair? No flame could have bridged such a gap. The Margate Fire Brigade had also performed experiments to prove that the burned parts of the carpet and the chair could only have been so burned by the application of a combustible such as petrol. A bottle of petrol had in fact been found in Sidney Fox's room, which he stated he was in the habit of using to clean his suit.

The matter of the insurance policies was brought into evidence as supplying motive. The expiration of the policies at midnight on 23 October 1929 and the accused's trip to extend them by only one day was highly suspicious. So, too, was the haste with which the accused made his claims against the policies while his mother lay as yet unburied in her coffin. Then, again, there was evidence in plenty of the accused's impecunious position – skipping various lodgings without settling his bill, forged cheques, petty frauds against tradesmen – all these pointed to a man so desperate for money that he would use extreme measures to remedy the situation.

All these witnesses took up the first four days of the trial, and on the fifth day Dr Roche Lynch, the Home Office pathologist, gave evidence of finding alcohol in the blood of the deceased consistent with her having consumed a half-bottle of port. The implication was that such a quantity would have induced a soporific state in the deceased which would have facilitated an act of murder by the accused although this was not overtly stated in the evidence. Lynch was immediately followed in the witness-box by Spilsbury.

Sir Bernard commenced his evidence by stating that his examination of the deceased had uncovered no significant heart disease or other disorder which could have accounted for sudden death from either heart failure or shock. She had suffered from Parkinson's disease, and there were other slight senile changes, but none which could have caused death. His next point concerned the absence of sooty deposits in the lungs or of carbon monoxide in the blood, thus ruling out suffocation as a cause of death.

He then came to the third and most crucial point in his evidence – that of finding the bruise at the back of the larynx. He gave his considered opinion that it had been caused by the breaking or tearing of small blood-vessels as a result of mechanical violence, consistent with manual strangulation. He had also found another smaller bruise on the tongue, most probably caused by pressure against the rear teeth during the act of strangulation: he could not account for it in any other way. He concluded by stating that he was fully convinced that Mrs Fox had died of manual strangulation, probably while in an alcohol-induced sleep, and certainly before the fire had started or there was any smoke in the room.

The defence hinged on the opinion of their pathologist, Dr Robert Brontë, that the bruise which Spilsbury had discovered behind the larynx was merely a post-mortem discoloration due to the setting in of putrefaction, but Spilsbury stuck to his guns. Unlike Dr Brontë, he had taken the precaution of making microscope slides of the tissue in question. The ensuing arguments were highly technical and from the layman's viewpoint boiled down to Dr Brontë trying to convince the jury that Spilsbury did not know a bruise from a post-mortem discoloration, but when Dr Brontë saw that here he was on a losing wicket he quickly went on to stress his contention that Mrs Fox had died of heart failure following shock at waking to find herself being strangled. This, too, was equally unlikely, and the doctor was forced to retire from the fray discomfited.

Sidney Fox was called to give evidence on his own behalf. Well-dressed in a natty outfit, dapper and well-groomed, his manner in the witness-box was cool and confident. His long story was a tissue of lies from start to finish, and unwittingly exposed his ruthless character mercilessly during cross-examination. One particular slip he made had a deadly effect on the jury. Asked by the Attorney-General how many doors his mother's room had, he said two – one communicating with his own room and one opening on to the corridor outside. Why, the Attorney-General continued relentlessly, after opening the communicating door to his own room and being driven back by billowing smoke, did he close the door again and then on his way to summon help on the intercom which was fastened to the wall in the corridor, close his own outer door and pass the door of his mother's room without opening it?

Fox's reply was unhesitating. 'So that the smoke should not spread into the hotel.' It would take little imagination to translate this to mean that, if he was unsure whether he had succeeded in his aim and his mother was in fact not yet dead, she should be left to suffocate for as long as possible. It is not known how long the fire had been burning before he summoned aid. Fox was in the witness-box for most of the seventh day of the trial, and the more he spoke the more he embroiled himself in the web of lies which was to prove his undoing. But at no time did he ever admit his crime, and he continued to show a confident façade to the world right to the end.

Whatever his outward manner, it was fairly clear that he was not confident as to the outcome of the trial; for he is one of the very few murderers who, after being sentenced to death, did not make any appeal. He must have known that he would have no chance at all of a reprieve.

Sidney Fox was hanged at Maidstone Prison on 8 April 1930.

6

A Passion for Hunting

Anchorage sounds like a safe harbour, a refuge from the storms that sweep the coast of Alaska, of which Anchorage is the state capital. But for twenty – possibly more – girls who came to America's far north from other parts of the country in search of work, it was anything but safe. One by one the girls disappeared, never to be seen again alive. All had become the victims of a man who had a passion for hunting.

The girls had sought work in a variety of professions. A number had capitalized on their assets of a shapely body, seemingly endless legs and firm, youthful breasts, and become dancers in topless establishments; a few had failed to make the grade in this highly competitive field and had drifted into the twilight world of prostitution.

The police, of course, knew that many of these girls were transients who had no home roots in Alaska, and several of them did not even use their real names, so when a girl went missing these two factors tended to impede any kind of police investigation: they literally did not know whom to start looking for. Frequently the drop-outs were reported missing only by some co-worker in the establishment where they were employed, and had no next of kin in the state.

Several girls had already gone missing by the beginning of 1980 but no one knew what had become of them. Not a single lead had been turned up by the police. But one day in 1980 some building workers were out on the Eklutna Road out of Anchorage, preparing the ground for some construction projects, when they came upon a shallow grave which had been partially-uncovered by marauding bears. The workmen were horrified to find exposed to view the naked corpse of a young woman, horribly mutilated by bears. She had once been an attractive blonde.

The police suspected that the body might be that of one of the missing girls, but they were unable to come up with any identification. All they had was the teeth, but identification could not be made from teeth without finding the girl's dentist. The body was too badly damaged to enable any cause of death to be established, nor was it possible to say whether the victim had been raped. The body was labelled and stored in the morgue in Anchorage, and very soon acquired the sobriquet of Eklutna Annie, from the location where she had been found.

A reporter named Harry S. Wheeler, who worked for one of Anchorage's big daily newspapers, decided to follow up the story of Eklutna Annie and see where it led. He knew that the police already had a dozen or so missing girls on their files, but none of their descriptions fitted the slender blonde who had been unearthed from her last resting-place on the remote Eklutna Road, which led straight out of Anchorage and on towards the remote icy wilderness of the Alaskan tundra.

The police were pretty sure that some of the missing girls had not just disappeared from the scene of their own accord but had met with foul play. A girl would not leave behind her clothes, jewellery, furs, or even her wages due from the establishment where she had been working as a stripper. She might not have worn very much on the stage, but she would most certainly have needed all her clothes when she left. It was cold outside, baby. Very cold.

The reporter checked with the manager of every stripjoint in Anchorage to try to ferret out the names and origins of the missing dancers. Most would not talk until Wheeler promised that no names or photographs would be used in his story. One manager summed up the situation for all of them when he said that when the girls came looking for work he never bothered to ask them for references, or where they had come from. 'Most of them don't even use their real names, so what's the point?' he said. 'I just tell the broads the rules of the house. No soliciting on the premises. No boozing until after they have finished their dance act. No touching the patrons or allowing the patrons to touch them. And that's it.'

The girls themselves, interviewed by Wheeler, were

equally tight-lipped until the reporter gave them the same guarantee of anonymity. 'Plenty of weirdos come in here,' one of them volunteered. 'They must be crackpots to come in here, pay through the nose for watered booze and know they're not allowed to touch, only look,' another said. A third girl interviewed said that patrons claiming to be photographers were often suspect. 'I was working in a joint in California before I came here,' she said, 'and one of my friends was hired by a so-called photographer to pose nude for a girlie mag – or so he told her. He got her into his car and took her to a house which he said was his place and induced her to pose in chains. She agreed to pose chained up for the pix he took, but – guess what? He kept her there chained up for a week! Knocked her about something awful – she was in hospital for a week.'

'Didn't she report it to the police?' the reporter asked. 'That's kidnapping!'

'Are you kidding!' the girl replied. 'She'd agreed to pose for money. She was a hooker. It turned out that the guy was some kind of big-shot. A media celebrity or something. The cops told her to forget it. They told her she was lucky they weren't going to book her for prostitution.'

Another girl told Wheeler that she had a rule: 'If a john offers me more than fifty bucks for going with him, forget it. It's the weirdos who flash a big wad to steer clear of. They're sure after something a lot more dangerous than just sex.'

Wheeler was learning a lot about topless dancers, hookers, girlie photographers and strip-joint life in Anchorage, but he had not found a single clue which would give a lead to the missing girls or to the fate which had befallen Eklutna Annie.

Two hunters were walking along the bank of the Knik River in a mountainous area a few miles from Anchorage on 12 September 1982. Their attention was attracted by the frenzied barking of their dog, and on going to investigate they discovered a shallow grave scooped out of the sandy soil. The nude corpse of a young woman lay surrounded by her clothes. These helped police to make a tentative identification, later to be confirmed from dental charts. The victim was a topless dancer named Sherry Morrow, aged twenty-three. Her boyfriend had reported the shapely brunette missing on 7 November 1981 – ten months earlier – after she failed to turn up to meet him after finishing her act at the bar where she appeared as a dancer. Her body was well-preserved, probably owing to the low temperatures over most of the year in the mountainous terrain where it had lain.

Anchorage police interrogated the boyfriend, the manager of the bar where the girl had worked, his staff, and other dancers she had known. No one could remember very much after such a long time, and no one could remember having seen her with anyone after leaving the bar. The body, however, provided a clue, revealed by the pathologist's report on the autopsy: the victim had been shot three times with a high-powered weapon. The investigators discovered shell casings, which appeared to have been dumped in the grave with the body and the victim's clothes. They proved to be from a high-velocity .223 calibre Ruger Mini-14 rifle. This is a very costly and unusual weapon firing a small slug but, being a repeater with a lot of firepower it is especially favoured by big-game hunters shooting at long-range targets. It wasn't the kind of weapon used by the average common-or-garden hunter going after short-range targets. Another point also emerged from the examination of the victim's clothes: there were no bullet holes. This indicated that the victim was nude when she was shot.

Hunting-rifles are not required to be registered in the USA and the weapon could have come from anywhere. It could have been purchased from any gunsmith who stocked this particular model. The police could not confiscate Ruger Mini-14s from their owners for a ballistics test without first obtaining a court order showing reasonable cause for the issue of a search warrant. And it was less than likely that the owner of the gun which killed Sherry Morrow would voluntarily hand it over for examination.

Another puzzle facing the investigators was the fact that the area where the body had been found was in remote and rugged terrain inaccessible to anything other than a specially-equipped vehicle, or perhaps a plane or helicopter. Even an average four-wheel-drive jeep without special adaptations would be unable to negotiate it. The killer had gone to a lot of trouble to reach the place.

The police were stymied. 'It sure isn't just a routine abduction case,' one officer said. 'I'd lay my bottom dollar that she was taken out there and killed there. Now why would anyone do that? There are plenty of easier places to abduct, rape and kill a woman. And weapons that would be easier to use, too ...'

Hunters find the area of the Knik River a good one for deer, moose, elk and bear. Two more hunters were in the area on 2 September 1983 (nearly a year later) when they stumbled upon another grave almost identical to the one found previously. The grave, shallowly scrabbled from sandy soil, contained another nude female body, clothes and shell casings from a Ruger Mini-14. Police identified the victim fairly quickly as Paula Golding, a twenty-two-year-old former secretary who had been made redundant from her job in the office of a fish cannery owing to a botulism scare which had closed a number of canneries in Anchorage.

Paula had applied for a job as a dance hostess in a bar. She was told she would have to dance topless. The manager of the bar told investigators: 'She was not like the usual run of broads we get. She was kinda shy and nervous. I asked her if she'd ever done this kind of work before and she said no, but she was desperate for work as she was out of a job and could not pay her rent or buy necessities. She seemed like a really nice girl. I told her to give it a try, but I could tell she felt a bit dubious about it. She worked for me for eight days and soon picked up the routine, but it wasn't really her thing. Then she disappeared. It was after her last shift, on 25 April. She didn't pick up her pay for the last two nights. I thought that mighty strange for a girl who was so desperate for money that she'd taken on the kind of job she'd never normally do. But then I figured she'd found another office job and didn't want to come back here even to pick up her two days' pay which was due. Like I said – she was a real nice kid – looked like the type who wouldn't even take off her bra in a girls' locker room. Used to blush at the least little thing.'

The bar manager had certainly been forthcoming, but leads to the murder of Paula Golding were not. The bar staff had no recall of seeing her with anyone either during working hours or as she left the bar, but this was hardly surprising in view of the strict rules about the dancers not being allowed to socialize with customers on the premises. So if Paula had met someone, it had been away from the bar and out of working hours. Some of the customers were traced, but few could remember much about a date six months prior to the body being found. It was a carbon copy of the Sherry Morrow case. The police hadn't got very far with that – and all they had to go on in this new case was that the victim had been shot in the nude with a Ruger Mini-14.

'It looks to me like someone has a thing about dancing girls,' said one officer. 'But who?'

'I'd lay my bottom dollar that there are more of them out there and that some of them would match the missing girl files,' a colleague replied. 'And I'll tell you something else. If we don't catch this creep soon, there'll be more.'

The proverbial looking for a needle in a haystack would pale into insignificance beside the notion of searching the vast Alaskan tundra around Anchorage for graves. If there were other graves they would only come to light if a hunter just happened to be in the area and came across them by chance. The only way the investigators had any opportunity of making any progress would be if they had an unexpected lucky break. And on 13 June they did.

Near midnight Officer Greg Baker was on patrol when he spotted a young girl running as fast as she could along the street with a handcuff dangling from one wrist, screaming hysterically. Baker pulled up level and bundled her into his car, holding her in his arms to calm her. Between sobs she gasped: 'He was going to kill me! I know he was going to kill me!' This was all he could elicit from her until she had been taken to police HQ, given a sedative by a police doctor, and was calm enough to make a coherent statement.

She told the officers that she was seventeen and admitted being a prostitute. She said she had picked up a man who had offered her 200 dollars for sex at his home, to which she agreed. Once there, in a big house in the affluent Muldoon district, he told her that they would have 'some fun and games' in the basement, as this could not be seen into from the outside.

In the basement, he locked the access door and told her to remove her clothes while he did likewise. Suddenly he snapped a handcuff on to one of her wrists, pushed her up against a supporting post and then snapped the cuff on her other wrist, securing her to the post. She asked him why he had done this considering that she was willing to engage in sex with him.

She soon realized why. He began a systematic series of tortures, to which she had definitely *not* agreed. Biting her nipples. Burning her body with cigarette ends. Thrusting the handle of a hammer into her vagina. She pointed out to him that she had agreed to normal sex, even oral sex, but not sadistic acts. He took no notice. When she screamed with pain he told her that no one could hear her from the basement of the house ...

Eventually he desisted. The girl by now was almost fainting from pain and shock. The man told her to dress and then handcuffed her to him. He told her that they were going to drive to a place where he kept a plane, in which they would go into the wilderness where he had a cabin. He told her that he had sometimes kept girls there for a week while he indulged in his peculiar forms of enjoyment with them. It was then that the girl knew she had to escape if she were to save her life from this maniac. He knew that she knew his address and what he looked like: he had never attempted to conceal his face.

When they reached the airfield where he kept his plane, he took off the handcuff that bound her to him and ordered her to climb up into the plane. Instead, she bolted and ran as fast as she could across the airfield. She was considerably younger than her abductor, whom she assessed as in his mid-forties, and easily outdistanced him. She calculated that she ran for about a mile before reaching an area of street lights and safety, where the man gave up the pursuit, but she kept on running until she ran into the arms of Officer Baker.

Asked for a description, the girl said that her abductor was thin and not very tall, about forty-five-ish. She said that his hair was reddish and thinning on top, that he was clean-shaven and wore horn-rimmed spectacles, and that his face was scarred and pockmarked. She also said that he had a stammer which was more marked when he became excited.

The officers left the girl with a policewoman and went into a huddle.

'Stutters? Pockmarked face? Red hair? Lives in Muldoon and has a private plane? That sounds like Bob Hansen to me!' one senior officer remarked.

'Yes, it sure does,' a colleague replied, 'but it can't be him! Why, he's one of the most respected citizens I can think of! He sure couldn't do anything like this. He must have a double.'

Robert Hansen, forty-four, owned a very successful bakery in Anchorage, where he had lived for seventeen years. He was well-known as a big-game and trophy hunter and had gained national recognition as being the first crossbowman to bag the famous Dall sheep in the Alaska mountains. As the police-officers said, he was the very last person anyone would suspect of kidnapping or assaulting young girls. But the description they had fitted him right down to the ground. If it wasn't him, then it had to be his identical twin.

The police drove the girl out to the Muldoon district and asked her to point out the house to which she had been taken, where she claimed she had been held prisoner, tortured and raped in the basement. The two officers accompanying her exchanged glances when she pointed out the home of Robert Hansen. Next, she was driven to Merrill Airfield, where a number of private planes are kept by some of Anchorage's wealthier citizens. The girl immediately pointed out a Piper Super Cub with oversized tyres specially made for landing and taking off in snow. It was Robert Hansen's plane.

The officers returned the girl to headquarters and went out to interview Hansen. He was at home and denied all knowledge of the matter. Asked to come to HQ, he accompanied the officers voluntarily. The girl immediately identified him as her assailant.

Hansen exploded with anger. 'She's lying through her teeth!' he stuttered. 'I can prove it!' And he went on to provide an alibi. He said he had spent the entire evening with two business acquaintances who had invited him to dinner to discuss commercial matters. He gave their numbers to the officers and invited them to call both these men, who confirmed Hansen's statement that he had spent the evening with them in the home of one of them and that he did not leave until some time after midnight. Both men were respected businessmen of the city. The police had no option but to let Hansen go.

'Now what are we going to do?' asked one bewildered police officer on reading the report next day. 'We have only the word of a teenage hooker, but I'd stick my neck out and bet that both Hansen's friends were lying. What we need is to be able to get a search warrant for a Ruger Mini-14 and get ballistics to check it out with the spent brass shell casings we have from the two graves.'

'Fat chance,' replied another officer. 'There's no way a prosecutor would file a charge without concrete evidence to put up against two prominent Anchorage businessmen, never mind Hansen himself.'

'Then what we have to do,' rejoined the first speaker, 'is to beat down on those two and get them to retract their statements giving Hansen his alibi.'

There was only one way to do that, and that was to go to the prosecutor and ask him to call a special grand jury hearing to interrogate the witnesses who would be called to testify. They would, by law, have to be warned that if they perjured themselves before a grand jury they could count on a two-year jail sentence, at the very least.

There was rejoicing among the police when their ploy worked. The two businessmen, appalled at the prospect of destroying their hard-won reputations and languishing for two years in prison, quickly retracted their statements even before being called as witnesses before the specially-convened grand jury hearing.

Both witnesses were told that, since they had not given their original statements under oath, no charges would be issued against them provided that they would voluntarily testify that Hansen had asked them to provide him with a false alibi, otherwise they could still be charged with attempting to obstruct justice.

The police now had Hansen's alibi in shreds and a positive identification by the young victim. A warrant was issued for his arrest, with search warrants for his home, car and plane, and even his bakery. The search turned up what the police most urgently wanted to find – a Ruger Mini-14 .223 calibre rifle. This was immediately handed over to ballistics for comparison with the shell casings from the graves.

As a bonus, the officers found an aviation map with twenty locations marked by asterisks. Two of these were along the Knik River and pinpointed the graves where the bodies of Sherry Morrow and Paula Golding had been found. Another marked the gravesite on the Eklutna Road where the corpse of the unknown woman known only as 'Eklutna Annie' had been discovered.

A fourth asterisk was near Seward, on the southern side of the Denai Peninsula, where the body of an unidentified woman had been found in a gravel pit in August 1980. This had not hitherto been connected with the murdered and missing girls from Anchorage. When the corpse had been discovered it had been partially-consumed by marauding bears. The victim had been shot in the head with a small-calibre weapon. The woman was eventually identified as Joanna Messina, who had been camping out in a tent with her dog while waiting for a cannery job. The dog had also been shot. The police finally learned that she had last been seen on 19 May 1980 talking to a man described as having reddish hair, a pockmarked face and horn-rimmed spectacles, who stuttered ...

With Hansen now in the custody of the Anchorage police, the state investigators requested an interview with the suspect at their own HQ. Hansen agreed to this and voluntarily waived his legal right to remain silent and to be represented by an attorney. Present at this interview were District Attorney Victor A. Krumm and his assistant Frank Rothschild, as well as two detective sergeants. The interview was recorded on tape over a two-day period.

Hansen began by announcing, 'Well, I guess you guys have got me on this charge of assaulting the young hooker. So what? She's just a whore. What do you guys want from me?'

'We'd like to talk to you about an aviation map we found at your place,' said one of the detectives, Glen Floyd. He spread the map out on the table before the suspect and pointed to the asterisked markings. 'Can you tell us about these marks?'

'Oh, I just mark places I've flown over,' said Hansen in a non-committal tone.

'We think the marks may have something to do with the graves of girls who have disappeared recently in this area,' Floyd replied.

'I don't know what you're talking about!' Hansen bluffed. 'Graves? What have those got to do with me?'

'Let's stop playing games,' District Attorney Krumm cut in. 'We've got your Ruger Mini-14 and our ballistics experts have positively identified it as the same gun that fired the shells found in the graves of the two women found buried near the Knik River. Do you want to tell us about that now, or do you want to wait until we book you for trial on murder charges?'

Hansen realized that he was trapped, and there was no avenue of escape, no loophole within the law. 'OK, you guys,' he said at last. 'I'll tell you.'

Twelve hours of tape were to spill out a mind-boggling story of incredible savagery. Even hardened police officers blanched as Hansen stuttered out his confession. The District Attorney and his assistant could scarcely believe it was happening. This was Robert Hansen, a man everyone in Anchorage had looked up to as a citizen to be proud of. How wrong could one be?

'Which was the first one you killed?' asked Krumm.

'The one in Seward,' Hansen replied. 'I'd abused women but I'd never killed one before. I was as sick as a dog when I got home. The reaction, I guess. But then I got to thinking more about how I had enjoyed the sense of power I had over her. I got more of a kick out of that than I did out of the sex. What a change from my younger days! In high school, no one would go out on a date with me because I stuttered and my face was scarred with acne. As I grew up I still stuttered and my face was permanently scarred with pockmarks. Women shunned me. I actually overheard one say to another, "I wouldn't be seen dead going out with that creepy-looking guy." So I started raping and abusing women. I'd show them I was just as good a man as one with a good voice and a clear complexion. I'd threaten them if they wouldn't do what I wanted. The sense of power that gave me made up for all those years of frustration when they had humiliated me.'

'Who was the second one you killed?' Krumm asked.

'That was the one you found out there on the Eklutna Road. Put up quite a fight, that one. Even drew a knife she had hidden in the top of her stocking. I'd picked her up on the street: she was just a whore. I don't know her name or where she came from. I never bothered to ask them their names. That second time, I didn't feel sick afterwards. And when I thought about it, it was more like the kind of feeling I'd get when I bagged a trophy animal. That's what these hookers were like: just animals. You couldn't respect them as fellow human beings. So I began fantasizing about hunting whores the same way I hunted caribou or bears.'

'How would you hunt them? After all, you already had them in your car,' the District Attorney suggested.

'When I stopped the car, or landed the plane, if we'd gotten that far, I demanded sex. I made them take off all their clothes. Then, afterwards, I'd turn them loose, stark naked. I'd been rough with them and they all wanted to escape. They'd take off running (some of them would have made good athletes, they had a fair turn of speed). I suppose those topless dancers would have been the most agile of the lot. I'd give them a good head start, then I'd come after them with the Mini-14. I'd let them see I was chasing them with the gun, and they'd run even faster, their bare boobs flopping about. Boy, that was the most exciting part of the chase. I'd take my time, like you do when you spot what you think might be a trophy-sized animal. Then I'd aim. But once you pull the trigger, it's over. All the thrill is in the chase, the stalking. I'd even let them think they'd got away – then I'd flush them out and start them running again.'

As Hansen recounted his story the interrogators listened in stunned amazement as their erstwhile model citizen related how he had stalked his nude victims like animals and finally killed them with long-range shots from his powerful weapon. After the recording session ended on the second day, Hansen was asked to go voluntarily with the state investigators in a police helicopter to pinpoint the marked gravesites on his map. The area was frozen and snow-covered, so the graves could not be uncovered until after the late spring thaw. He agreed to go. 'There's a blonde down there,' he said at one point; the redhead 'with the biggest boobs you ever saw' was said to be buried at another location. In all, sixteen sites were logged.

After the confession, Hansen's attorney called upon the District Attorney to plea-bargain that his client was willing to plead guilty to the four murders in which the bodies had been found, and also to counts of rape and kidnapping, provided that later murder charges were not filed after more bodies had been located. Krumm said that he would give him an answer after conferring with the trial judge. Since there is no capital punishment in Alaska, the most Hansen could receive was life imprisonment without possibility of parole. If Hansen were given the maximum sentence on the four cases, there would be no point in charging him with further murders, incurring additional expense and a lengthy trial, since it was unlikely that he would ever be released.

At a second meeting with the defence attorney Krumm said that he would accept the four guilty pleas and not file additional murder charges later. But he stipulated that the additional rape and kidnapping charges must stand. Hansen's attorney had one more request, that his client wanted to serve his sentence in a prison outside Alaska. He was fearful that the boyfriend of one of his victims might perchance be sent to the same prison for some offence and would kill him. The District Attorney, doubtless with some degree of sarcasm, pointed out that a man who had on his own admission killed twenty women was hardly in a position to be overly concerned about saving his own life. But he agreed to the request anyway.

On Monday, 28 February 1984, Robert Hansen stood trial before Judge Ralph Moody, in a courtroom packed with spectators and reporters from newspapers all over America. Prosecutor Krumm came straight to the point as he outlined the charges: 'Your Honour, before you sits a monster, an extreme aberration of a human being, a man who has walked among us for seventeen years selling us doughnuts, Danish and coffee, with a pleasant smile on his face. That smile concealed crimes that would numb the mind ... I have heard in his own words how he raped more than thirty women and how he killed at least twenty – and possibly more. I have heard him tell how he held a gun to their heads with the threat to kill them if they did not go along with every act he demanded.

'This meek-looking man who has lived among us for so many years is a hunter, a bowman who has won awards for bagging caribou, moose, bear and Dall sheep. He relished his power over animals, not for the food they provided but for his prowess as a hunter. But that was not enough. He chose to put young women in the role of animals. He turned them loose nude and hunted them down with his gun. It was all a game for him: done for thrills, at the expense of human life.

'This hunter, this man who kept trophy heads of animals mounted on the walls of his home, now has trophies scattered throughout south-eastern Alaska in the graves that hold the bodies of young women ... How many we don't know. We are sure only of twenty and we will not know *who* they are until we can find all the graves. Not even in his twisted mind did he keep a record of who they were; he recalls them only by the size of their breasts, or by some vicious act he committed upon them before killing them.

'The state of Alaska asks for the maximum penalty that the law allows for each of the charges, to which he has entered a plea of guilty.'

Judge Moody then announced that he was imposing a life sentence for one of the murder charges, sentences of ninety-nine years each on the other three murder charges, plus forty years for the rape charges and a further forty years for kidnapping, all the sentences to run consecutively. Hansen would not be eligible for parole for 461 years, which meant in effect that he could never be released. After passing sentence, the judge addressed all those in the courtroom: 'I hope that when I leave this courtroom today,' he said, 'I have ensured that this man will never again walk the streets of America – or anywhere else.'

Hansen was transported to prison in an undisclosed location in another state, the identity of which was also a closely-guarded secret. As he travelled, handcuffed to a guard on either side, one wonders what he was thinking.

Was he remembering how he had handcuffed young girls to himself? Did he now realize how they had felt? Or were his sensibilities too blunted?

One thing was certain: the topless dancers in the Anchorage strip-joints, and even the prostitutes who pounded the streets, were now able to breathe freely once more, now that the man with a passion for hunting had been finally caged.

7
The Fatal Slip

The engaged couple seemed the ideal pair. Elsie Cameron was the twenty-six-year-old daughter of respectable parents who lived in Maida Vale, London, and Norman Thorne, two years younger, was a self-employed chicken farmer who had lived in Kensal Rise (another London suburb) but now owned a piece of land at Blackness, near Crowborough in Sussex, where he had established his business, the Wesley Poultry Farm.

Elsie had met Norman at her local church in 1920, which he also attended. There he was a Sunday-school teacher, a Band of Hope member and an assistant scoutmaster with the troop attached to the church. Elsie was a typist in a local firm of electrical engineers. She was small and slender, just this side of pretty, shy and modest in manner and wore gold-rimmed spectacles. Even so, despite her disarmingly quiet mien, it was she who made most of the running where Norman was concerned. She was a very determined young woman beneath the diffident exterior, and one of the things she was most determined to do was to marry the young man of her choice. Even her parents agreed with her that a man with his initiative in business would be a better prospect than some of the other young men they knew who were content to plod along for years clerking in some dimly-lit warehouse or in a similar dead-end job.

Norman had started his career as an electrical engineer with Fiat Motors' depot in Wembley. He was the son of an engineer who was an inspector for the Admiralty. In March 1918 Norman joined the Royal Naval Air Service as a mechanic and was sent to Belgium, where he suffered concussion from the blast of a bomb. After the war ended he was demobbed and again resumed his trade of mechanic in civilian life. But, along with thousands of others, he was forced to go on the dole in the summer of 1921 when employment in his chosen sphere was at a premium.

Norman Thorne was not a man to acquiesce lightly in the face of this blow to his self-esteem. He persuaded his father to lend him a hundred pounds, with which on 22 August 1921 he bought a piece of land to set up his farm. To start with he lodged in the nearby village while building the requisite housing for his stock, cycling home every weekend. Then, to save money, having installed laying hens in the brood houses, day-old chicks in the incubators and secure rat-proof housing for stockfeed, he decided to adapt one of the brood houses into a hut to live in. It was a modest 12-foot by 8-foot hut and housed a folding bed, portable cooker, a table and two chairs, hooks on the wall for coats and a curtained-off corner rail for his other clothes with shelves for the smaller items. There was even a rug on the floor. The observer would not have believed that it had originally been intended to house hens.

Once Norman was established in his new abode, he spent far less time travelling to his London home at weekends; that was the object of the exercise in the first place. Money previously spent on railway fares would be more profitably ploughed back into the business. He was not doing too badly with new-laid eggs, although trussed chickens for the oven took a bit longer and also brought less profit owing to the weeks of feeding. Elsie now began visiting him at the hut, travelling by train at weekends. She spent the days with him there, but stayed the nights in lodgings in the village. At Christmas 1922 they announced their formal engagement.

Elsie had been nine years with the engineering firm where she worked, but soon after her engagement was announced she became forgetful and moody, and her employers had no option but to give her notice as her efficiency was very much impaired. A pity, they told her, but an absent-minded person constantly immersed in daydreams was no use in the office. She quickly obtained another job, but the same thing happened again; and in fact she obtained and subsequently lost three other jobs

after this one, all on the grounds of her apparent change of
mental attitude. She now turned her full attention to the
one thing that would absolve her from the necessity of
going out to work: marriage to her fiancé. She could help
him with feeding the chickens and so on as well as the
more usual domestic tasks.

Both her brother and her sister married in 1923, but
Norman, she noted, seemed surprisingly reluctant to
name the day where she was concerned, despite some
pointed references when she acted as a bridesmaid at the
weddings of both her siblings. Norman feigned an
ignorance he probably did not have of what she was
talking about, and continued his stolid indifference to her
veiled hints. She now decided to be a bit more
forthcoming and wrote him some letters, full of
endearments but also mentioning straight out that
marriage was on her mind, and soon. Here she was
pushing thirty and still on the shelf, despite being
engaged.

The chicken farm was meanwhile not prospering as it
should, and Norman was in debt. This was scarcely the
time to contemplate marriage, he told her, to which she
replied that love in a hut was still love just as love in a
palace, and she could manage. He did not see it that way,
and made the usual excuse that he preferred to postpone
the ceremony until such time as he could offer her a more
secure future.

By the spring of 1924 Norman's already waning interest
had been fragmented still further by his meeting with a
bright and extrovert young girl named Elizabeth Coldicott,
known as Bessie, who was a dressmaker and lived in the
village. He had met her at a local dance, and they began
keeping company during the week, in order to avoid Elsie
(who came only at weekends) getting to know what her
two-timing fiancé was up to. Meanwhile Elsie's mental
condition had been steadily deteriorating, so that instead
of being merely listless and depressed she now frequently
became hysterical and even abusive. Norman took her to a
local doctor, who diagnosed 'nerves' and prescribed
sedatives.

At the end of October Elsie, by now desperate, informed
Norman that she was pregnant. Norman, however, was

sceptical, pointing out to her that he had always 'been careful' (the euphemism current at that time for *coitus interruptus*). She in turn was quick to inform him that even 'being careful' was not one hundred per cent foolproof (as many a young girl both before and since has learned to her dismay). It was subsequently proved that she was not pregnant; it had been merely a ploy to induce her fiancé to marry her with all haste.

In an attempt to convince him she met him at Groombridge (between Crowborough and Tunbridge Wells) and talked repeatedly of her 'pregnancy', urging him to fix a wedding date and call the banns in Tunbridge Wells. But Norman still put her off, using every plausible excuse in the book. His real reason was that he had fallen in love with Bessie Coldicott, whom he was now seeing every night from Monday to Friday. He found her warm and understanding and a great deal more fun than the mentally-disturbed Elsie, who was by turns apathetic and lethargic or hostile and given to screaming. He decided to pacify Elsie sufficiently to send her home, and then write her a letter, which read in part:

> You seem to be taking everything for granted. I shall not be going to Tunbridge Wells this week ... There are one or two things I haven't told you about ... It concerns someone else ... I am afraid that I am between two fires.

On 26 November Elsie replied:

> Certainly I take everything for granted ... and I shall expect you to go and arrange our marriage as soon as possible ... This worry is very bad for the baby ... I feel sick every day, and things will soon be noticeable to everybody. I want to be married before Christmas. I really do think an explanation is due to me over all this.

The next day Norman replied:

> What I haven't told you is that I have met another girl ... She thinks I am going to marry her, of course, and I have a strong feeling for her ...

On 28th November Elsie wrote back:

I gave you myself and all my love, and you have
deceived me ... You are engaged to me and I have first
claim on you. You don't write a single word of love to
me, and I have stood by you through all your
unemployment and farm troubles ... I expect you to
finish with the other girl, and to marry me as soon as
possible. My baby must have a name, and another
thing, I love you in spite of everything ... I have often
been told that you can't trust any man, but oh, Norman,
I thought you were different.

On Sunday, 30 November, Elsie arrived at the farm just
before 11 a.m. uninvited. She was in one of her
all-too-frequent aggressive moods. 'Who is this other girl?'
she demanded. 'Why haven't you gone to Tunbridge
Wells? When are we going to be married?'

Norman did his best to pacify her yet again. His excuse
this time was that he could not set a date until he had first
sorted things out – mainly financial – with his father.
'After all,' he said, 'we can't marry without any money.'

Elsie, though mollified, was still suspicious. She left the
farm at 7.50 p.m. and caught the 8.18 p.m. train from
Crowborough back to her home in London. Norman,
having seen her safely off, returned to the farm in time to
welcome Bessie Coldicott at 8.30 p.m. He told her of his
dilemma, and she was understanding and sympathetic.
They decided that the best thing would be for Norman to
invite his father for a discussion of his problems, and three
days later his father called at the hut. They chatted about
Norman's financial vicissitudes and about his fiancée, and
the elder Thorne suggested that if his son really had
doubts about the supposed pregnancy he should wait
until after Christmas before committing himself to any
marriage plans. By that time it would become more
obvious whether Elsie really was pregnant or not.

Norman wrote to Elsie informing her that his father had
been to the farm to talk things through, and on receipt of
this letter Elsie decided it was high time she went to the
farm to settle matters with Norman once and for all. She
made herself as attractive as possible with a new hair-do, a
green wool dress and new shoes. In a suitcase she carried
some spare clothing, including a new jumper, and some

baby clothes she had knitted. She was fully prepared to stay with Norman in the hut until such time as she had personally accompanied him to Tunbridge Wells to post the banns. He had told her that his father had given him some money, so there was now no excuse he could give her. She must have been optimistic as to the outcome of her mission as, according to one of her mother's lady lodgers, Elsie was whistling as she left the house at about two o'clock on the afternoon of Friday, 5 December. Having spent what little money she had saved on her new outfit, after she had paid her single fare to Crowborough she had only three-halfpence left in her purse. Still, not to worry. Norman would be taking care of her from now on ...

Five days later her father was wondering what had happened to her. Never before had she not returned on Sunday night after visiting her fiancé at his farm. Mr Cameron sent him a telegram on 10 December reading:

ELSIE LEFT FRIDAY STOP HAVE HEARD NO NEWS STOP HAS SHE ARRIVED STOP PLEASE WIRE BY RETURN – CAMERON

Norman Thorne's reply came by return:

ELSIE NOT HERE STOP CANNOT UNDERSTAND – THORNE

Mr Cameron waited one more day in case his daughter should turn up. Then he reported her missing to the police.

On 12 December PC Beck was detailed to visit the farm and interview the chicken farmer to see what light he could shed on the girl's mysterious disappearance. The helpful fiancé gave PC Beck a photograph of Elsie, and was asked to call at Crowborough police station the following day to make a statement.

In his statement, Norman Thorne said that on the Friday (5 December) he had cycled to Tunbridge Wells at about 1.30 p.m. and purchased a pair of shoes and a chess set with part of the money his father had given him. He returned home at about 3.45 p.m. fed his chickens and went to buy some milk from a neighbouring farmer. He then had his tea. He was in his hut, he said, from about 5 p.m. to about 9.45 p.m., when he went to Crowborough railway station to meet Miss Coldicott and her mother, who had been on a day trip to Brighton and he had arranged to meet them off the train and escort them home as the road was unlit, after which he went home at about 11.30 p.m.

The next day, his statement continued, was Saturday and he went to Groombridge railway station where he anticipated meeting Elsie, who had written to him asking him to meet her there at 11 a.m. There was no sign of his fiancée, and after waiting around to see if she would be arriving on a later train, he took the next train to Tunbridge Wells, where he made a few food purchases, and then returned home. He then went as usual to fetch milk from the neighbouring farm, and in the evening went to the cinema with Miss Coldicott. The next day he wrote to Elsie: 'Where did you get to yesterday?'

Much of this was confirmed by the police. But they had also found a couple of witnesses – two gardeners going home after work – who had seen her, complete with attaché-case, walking in a purposeful manner along the road which led to the chicken farm on 5 December. The time had been around 5.15 p.m.

In the meantime the ever-helpful Norman was showing police and newspaper reporters around his farm, explaining proudly how he had built up the business from a small loan from his father. He invited both police and reporters into his converted hen-house home, showing them all the improvements he had made for his own comfort. He talked freely, posing for photographs with his dog, and also in one of the runs feeding the chickens. Questioned once more, he was quite categorical in his denial that Elsie had ever arrived at the farm, either on 5 December or afterwards. The two gardeners were mistaken, he averred, without batting an eyelid.

On New Year's Day of 1925 Norman wrote to Bessie Coldicott, his new love: 'Looking back over the last few months, I perceive many changes in my life ... She [Elsie] had a strange disposition, and even her parents tried to force her on me ... Lately she has made my life a misery with her continual demands ... I don't want you to worry about it any more, love. I cannot let her stand in the way of our happiness. I must stop her somehow. I will find a way.'

A month passed, and the police were still interviewing witnesses who might throw some light, however feebly flickering, on the strange disappearance of Elsie Cameron. In desperation the local police called in Scotland Yard, and eventually Chief Inspector Gillan was appointed to head the investigation. It was not long before he located a bus inspector who had seen Elsie on 5 December at a small local bus depot, carrying a small brown attaché-case and fitting the description circulated. The girl had inquired of him about the buses, saying she wished to get to Blackness, near Crowborough. It was a Saturday night, he said, and later when he saw pictures of the missing girl in the newspapers he remembered remarking to his wife that it was the same girl who had asked him about the buses.

Chief Inspector Gillan next located the driver of the bus the girl had boarded. Cecil Copplestone, too, remembered the occasion. 'The bus inspector had seen her on to my bus,' the driver related, 'and as there was hardly anyone on the bus she came and sat as near the cab as she could and we got talking. I remember she said she'd come from London but would much rather live in the country, and was hoping to move to this area soon.' Inspector Gillan showed him a photograph of Elsie Cameron. 'Why, that's her!' the bus driver said. 'I'd know her anywhere. Had a sweet sort of smile, she did. I remember something else, too – she had some fancy sort of shiny hair slides in her hair. I let her off the bus as near Blackness as we went, and she started walking down the lane in the direction of the farm.'

While Chief Inspector Gillan deployed men to search the nearby Ashdown Forest, he himself decided to pay Norman Thorne a visit. 'We're still no nearer to finding Miss Cameron,' the inspector told him. 'Perhaps you may have some new ideas?'

'I'm delighted that Scotland Yard have been called in at last!' the chicken farmer enthused. 'These local police haven't come up with a thing.'

'I'm sure they've done their best,' replied Gillan.

Norman invited him into the hut. 'Maybe she'll be found now,' he said. 'You know, both her mother and I think that she's being held somewhere against her will. Kidnapped, you know.'

'You don't think that maybe she had met another man and they have gone off quietly somewhere?' asked the inspector tentatively.

'Most unlikely!' Norman said passionately. 'Why, Inspector – we were engaged to be married!'

'So I understand,' the policeman said tersely.

'She would never even have looked at another man,' Norman continued. 'Of course, she'd always been used to living in London and it's a bit quiet out here, so she was wondering how she'd get used to the change. But I'd managed to convince her.'

'Do you mind if I take a look around your place?' he said. 'I've never visited a pedigree chicken farm – only ever seen the common-or-garden variety in backyards.'

Norman Thorne was an enthusiastic breeder and led the older man around his premises with alacrity. 'In three weeks' time,' he said, 'I'll have a thousand eggs in those incubators. Pedigree RIR.'

'What's RIR?'

'Rhode Island Red. One of the best breeds for brown eggs. Sell well round here.'

'Well, thanks for showing me round,' Gillan said. 'I'll let you know if we find out anything new.' Norman escorted him to the gate and waved a friendly goodbye as the police car drove off.

The very next morning the inspector was back. Norman appeared delighted. 'Good news, I hope?' he queried. 'You found something out yesterday?'

'Not after I left here,' the inspector replied. 'Do you mind if a few of my men take another look around?'

Norman objected abruptly. 'I didn't mind showing *you* around, Inspector,' he said, 'but I can't allow four or five men to go trampling about. It will make the hens nervous, and you'd be surprised what that does to their egg-laying. Sorry.'

'We'll be as careful as we can,' Gillan replied. 'I'm sorry, but we have to make a more thorough search.'

'What can you possibly hope to find here?' Norman said

in a voice that betrayed that it was he who was nervous rather than his laying stock. 'You've no right on my land anyway. I showed *you* over the place yesterday as a courtesy.'

'We've got every right,' Gillan said. 'We've even got a search warrant. So let's get started and get it over with. Lead the way.'

The policemen followed Norman from house to house, tapping floorboards, looking carefully for any signs that flooring had been recently removed or replaced, boards prised up, irregular surfaces. Bags and sacks of layers' mash, cracked wheat, oyster-shell grit and day-old chick mash was examined.

The police then moved to the hen-house which Thorne had turned into a home. On a table was an unfinished letter to Bessie Coldicott. In an Oxo tin on a shelf was Elsie's wristwatch, a bracelet and two pairs of ear-rings, and a ring. And behind the makeshift curtained 'wardrobe' were two ladies' dresses and a coat as well as the various items of male apparel.

'She kept some clothes and things here,' Thorne offered lamely. 'She didn't want her parents to know that she stayed here.'

'Never mind all that. Where is the girl now?'

'I don't know! You're the police – you find her! I don't know where she is!'

Gillan gave Thorne the usual caution, and at 3.30 p.m. on 14 January 1925 he was arrested and taken to Crowborough police station while the police detachment continued their search of the premises. By 4 p.m. it was too dark to see, and the search resumed the following day. At 8 a.m. men arrived with picks, shovels and spades and began to dig.

At 8.25 a.m. PC Adrian Philpott struck a hard object with his spade. A sodden brown attaché-case was unearthed, bearing the initials E.C. Inside were two towels, a number of baby garments, a new crêpe dress, a new red jumper, a blouse and skirt, changes of underwear, a pair of embroidered silk pyjamas, a pair of gold-rimmed spectacles and a few toiletries and make-up items. The case and its contents were conveyed to the police station and shown to Norman Thorne, who agreed that they were the property of his missing fiancée. He still professed no knowledge of the girl's whereabouts. Asking why he was being detained, he was told that he had been arrested on suspicion of being concerned with Elsie's disappearance, and for good measure the police officer added that if and when her body was found he might be charged with murder.

Digging continued despite the January cold and the incessant drizzle, while Gillan toiled unremittingly in another direction – the location and interviewing of more witnesses. On applying to a Crowborough labour exchange for some unemployed navvies to help with the heavy digging in the frozen ground of the farm, Gillan had an unexpected stroke of luck. A labourer told him that about a month previously he and some of his mates had done a job for Norman Thorne on his farm, moving his biggest brood house to a new site. 'The land becomes sour if you keep a house in one place too long,' the man explained. 'You have to move them every so often to rest the ground and give it a chance to recover.'

'Can you remember where the house stood before you moved it?' the policeman asked.

'Sure – it was over there,' the man replied, pointing.

'We'll move it back,' Gillan said, 'and start digging in the ground under the present site.' It took all the strength of ten men to shift the heavy structure thirty feet. The disturbed hens squawked madly with indignation.

The afternoon light was fading fast. Gillan ordered floodlights to be brought in from London – no source nearer was available but they arrived with exemplary celerity. The atmosphere was tense, filled with the rhythmic clang of shovels and picks against winter-hardened earth, accompanied by the soft putter of generators in the background. The earth beneath where the brood house had lately stood was, of course, much softer and easier to dig than that in the more exposed situations, owing to its having been protected from the worst of the elements while it had remained *in situ*.

Chief Inspector Gillan's hunch paid off. Fairly soon after digging had commenced in this area, the workmen pulled a heavy burlap sack to the surface. As they did so the neck of the sack fell open to reveal a delicate white female hand, manicured with coral nail varnish. Two policemen opened the remainder of the sack to disclose to their horrified gaze a headless torso. A young PC and one of the workmen vomited at the sight. Nevertheless, digging continued by those with stronger stomachs and a second sack came to light. This contained the girl's head, the face badly bruised, the wavy blonde hair still held by marcasite hair slides, one on each side. Further investigation of this second sack revealed a pair of legs, crudely hacked from the body, at the bottom, bent at the knees to fit into their coarse burlap shroud. One of the workmen fled the scene: it was just too much.

Norman Thorne was charged with the murder of Elsie Cameron and sent for trial at Lewes Assizes on 4 March 1925 before Mr Justice Finlay. Sir Henry Curtis-Bennett led for the Crown, and Thorne was defended by Mr J.D. Cassels KC. The accused had put forward a defence that he thought would be hard either to prove or disprove; that Elsie had committed suicide in his hut while he was out and that when he returned he found her body, panicked and disposed of it. He fully admitted dismembering it and burying it under some spare ground on his plot, then moving the large brood house to its new site over the grave, but he denied killing the unfortunate girl to the end.

In his statement he said that Elsie had arrived in a belligerent mood, saying that 'she had come to stay with me in the hut until we were married'. He went out at about 7.30 p.m. to see if a neighbouring family would put her up for the night, as he did not think it proper that she should stay with him, but she was adamant, and the neighbours were out anyway and he did not see them. Thorne and his fiancée then had one of their frequent arguments, which continued until supper-time. At about 9.30 p.m. he said he had to go to the railway station to meet Miss Coldicott and her mother. This started another argument about his association with Miss Coldicott. When he left for the railway station he thought that Elsie would hve calmed down by the time he returned at about 11.30 p.m.

On arriving at the hut, his statement continued, he saw

that the door was open and the dog ran down the path to meet him, which he thought was strange. He went in and was horrified to see Elsie hanging from a beam by a length of washing-line. 'I cut her down,' he continued, 'and laid her on the bed. She was dead ... I sat thinking, I ought to go and fetch the doctor and then go for the police. But then I realized the position I would be in if she were found at my place dead ...' He then went on to detail how he had dismembered the body and taken it out for burial, and later hired some workmen to help him move the brood house over the spot. He also described how Elsie's father had telegraphed him when she did not return home, and how he had wired back to say that she had never arrived – a fiction which he was to persist in until such time as the police discovered her body.

The forensic evidence took up most of the trial and, as so often happens, the medical experts disagreed as to the cause of death. Sir Bernard Spilsbury, after explaining that the severe winter conditions had preserved the body to a remarkable degree so that decomposition was barely discernible, declared that the girl had been beaten to death and that there were no signs of hanging. Bruising was apparent on her face, shoulders, chest, abdomen and one leg, as well as blunt trauma to the head, all of which had been caused before death. One head injury he described as having been 'a crushing blow with a club or similar implement'. Another blow to the back of the head, causing trauma to the base of the brain, was the blow that killed her, but, he said, even without this some of the other blows had been so severe that the beating would have been fatal anyway.

The experts agreed that Elsie Cameron had died between one and a half and two hours after she had consumed a light meal, and that her body had been dismembered not less than five and not more than seven hours after death. She had not been pregnant either then or at any previous time.

The chief medical witness for the defence, Dr Robert Brontë, said that he had found rope marks on the victim's neck, but Spilsbury contended that the crease marks on the neck were of the kind that naturally occurred on most well-built persons' necks. It was decided that the best way of resolving the controversy was to examine the beam from which Elsie was supposed to have hanged herself. The beam, examined *in situ* in the hut by the police earlier, was very dusty, and the police testified that no marks had been found in the dust suggesting that a rope had been tied around it. Now the beam was to be produced in court having been sawn from its moorings for the purpose.

It was put forward that if a person weighing 120 pounds (Elsie had weighed eight stone eight pounds) were to be hanged on a rope from the beam there would be a dent in the wood at the point where the rope had encircled it. The jurors examined the beam from end to end, and there was no dent in the wood at any point in its length. The beam was now fixed to supports and a 120-pound weight suspended from it at various points by a rope similar to the one used as a washing-line on Thorne's farm. A dent was made in the wood at every point where the weight was suspended. The conclusion which was inevitably drawn from this was that no girl weighing 120 pounds – eight stone eight pounds – had ever hanged herself from that beam. Despite the incontrovertible evidence, Thorne stuck doggedly to his story of the suicide by hanging. 'Why should I kill her?' he asked. 'I loved her. We were going to be married.'

The prosecution were quick to point out that Elsie had become a nuisance and stood in the way between the accused and Miss Coldicott and that it was in fact Miss Coldicott that he wished to marry. At this point Miss Coldicott was called as a witness, and it was she who was able to provide proof that Norman Thorne had intended to kill Elsie Cameron and that it had in fact been a premeditated murder.

Bessie Coldicott had kept all Norman's letters, including the one he had written to her on 1 January 1925 containing the sentence 'I cannot let her stand in the way of our happiness. *I must stop her somehow. I will find a way.*' Note those italicized words. They are the clearest indication that Norman Thorne was prepared to go to any lengths, even murder, to remove the obstacle from his path. Writing those words was his fatal slip. Many a murderer commits just one fatal error, and that was the one that convicted Norman Thorne, far more telling than a dusty plank which could not sustain the weight of a suicide without indenting its surface.

The jurors were out for less than half an hour before coming up with a unanimous verdict of guilty of murder. He lodged an appeal, which was rejected out of hand. A letter he wrote from prison to his parents read in part: 'They say a man has to be *proved* guilty; in what way was it proved against me? What happened while I was out I do not know.'

Norman Thorne was hanged at Wandsworth Prison on 22 April 1925. If the unfortunate Elsie had lived, it would have been her twenty-seventh birthday.

8

The Fiery Furnace

Hawley Crescent, in London's Camden Town, is today most notable for being the site of the studios of TV-am. But fifty-five years ago it was just one of the many undistinguished streets of that suburb, situated just north of the present underground station and containing clusters of terraced houses separated by the various smaller streets that opened off on either side.

In one of these houses, number 30, lived a man named Thomas John Wynne, a Welshman who had come some years earlier from his native Caernarvon to seek work in London. He had found nothing more glamorous than a mundane and repetitive factory job, and eked out his meagre wages by letting one or two rooms to lodgers and also renting a shed in his backyard to a builder and decorator for storing his tools and materials and for use as an office.

On the evening of Tuesday, 3 January 1933, Mr Wynne was just about to leave home for his favourite pub when he spotted a red glow in his backyard and saw to his horror that the shed he rented to the builder and decorator was ablaze. Knowing the danger from inflammable materials such as paint, turpentine and softwood he made all haste to call the fire brigade. After firemen had extinguished the flames they discovered the charred body of a man seated on a high stool at the office desk. The builder and decorator's name was, appropriately enough, Samuel Furnace. He lived in Crogsland Road, about 500 yards from Hawley Crescent, a married man with five children, the eldest of whom was a ten-year-old-boy. He was a native of St Neots in Huntingdonshire and had pursued an adventurous career, having been a ship's steward and then subsequently serving in the Rifle

Brigade and with the Black and Tans. Now self-employed, he was finding the building and decorating business somewhat precarious and was known to have financial problems.

No one was very surprised, then, when a suicide note was found near the body. It was brief and to the point: 'Goodbye, all. No work and no money. Sam J. Furnace.' Poor old Sam must have given up the unequal struggle, his family, friends and neighbours said – but some added, 'What a way to die – there must have been any number of easier ways if he was determined to commit suicide.' It was true; very few suicides choose self-immolation as the method. It must be very painful indeed to be cooked alive.

Mr Bentley Purchase, the coroner, was one of those who suspected even more strongly that this was not suicide. For one thing, suicide notes are usually rather less terse and brief, and they are usually addressed to someone – a parent, a friend or even the police. And for another thing, although most of the contents of the hut were badly damaged by the fire and the body was charred beyond recognition, the suicide note was clean and neatly folded and had escaped damage. It looked just as if someone had put it there afterwards. Finally, the coroner decided that he would personally attend the post-mortem by the Home Office pathologist and examine the body himself.

His misgivings were not without foundation. The post-mortem revealed that the charred body had been shot twice in the back with a small calibre weapon, and that the man had been dead before the fire started. Examination of the teeth revealed that they could not possibly be the teeth of a man of forty-two, which was Furnace's age. They were the teeth of a much younger man – a man between twenty and thirty.

Meanwhile the police had been busy and had searched the partially-burnt-out shed in Mr Wynne's backyard. This had revealed an overcoat hanging on a hook, in the pocket of which was a Post Office Savings' Bank book bearing the name of Walter Spatchett. Spatchett was a twenty-five-year-old rent collector employed by a firm of estate agents called Westacott and Son, of Camden Road, Camden Town, and lived with his parents in Dartmouth Park Road, Highgate. He was last seen on the evening of 3

January prior to the fire, at which time, his employers calculated, he would have had at least £40 on him from the collection of rents. He knew Samuel Furnace, since Mr Wynne employed Westacott's to collect the rents of his tenants, even though they rented premises or lodged at his own house, so as to keep the tenancies on a business footing. There was much less likelihood of tenants falling behind with their rents by keeping to such an arrangement. Of course the estate agents charged a small commission for their services, but Mr Wynne considered this a small price to pay to avoid any hassle over non-payment.

The alleged suicide note was shown to Spatchett's parents, who stated categorically that it was not in their son's handwriting, and anyway: why would he have signed such a note in the name of Furnace? It now seemed pretty obvious to the police that Furnace had killed Spatchett and staged the mock suicide, setting fire to the shed in order to destroy the body and thus avoid its identification. Unfortunately for him, his plan misfired. How often murderers imagine that they can put one over on the police, frequently because they are not privy to the secrets of the forensic pathology laboratory such as those that were crucial in this case! As we have already seen in the case of Sidney Fox (*see* Chapter 5), the dead cannot inhale smoke, so Samuel Furnace would have been unlikely, as a layman of limited education, to have known about the tests for carbon monoxide in the blood or soot deposits in the lungs; neither is he likely to have known that an adult of twenty-five has different characteristics in his teeth from those of an adult of forty-two. Then, too, Furnace was incredibly careless; he left an overcoat belonging to his victim hanging on a peg in the shed with a bank book in the pocket which provided perfect identification of the victim. And surely nobody would write a suicide note like that!

Forty pounds would not, perhaps, go very far these days but to Sam Furnace it meant a great deal. With the value of money what it was in those days, he would have been able to settle his debts and start a new life somewhere else. However, he did not get very far before Nemesis, in the shape of the police, caught up with him. A

nation-wide hue and cry was put out for him, and
'sightings' of him were reported from all over Britain. On 9
January an appeal was broadcast by BBC radio.
Eventually, he was traced to Southend-on-Sea, where he
booked in as 'Mr King' in a modest boarding-house near
the railway station. He kept to his room, going out only for
meals (he had requested only bed and breakfast because
he feared meeting the other guests at lunch or dinner who
might recognize him from newspaper photographs, but
was able to take breakfast in his room, saying that he had
been ill). He also went out for newspapers, and to post a
letter to his brother-in-law asking for help – a very unwise
move, for his brother-in-law took it straight to the police.
Here is part of the letter Furnace wrote. (I have amended
this slightly to remove the original spelling and
grammatical errors.)

> I am in Southend, quite near the railway station, making
> out I have been ill with the 'flu. Actually I am far from
> well through want of sleep – I don't think I have slept
> one hour since the accident happened.
>   Now what I want you to do is not for me but for May
> and the kiddies. My days are numbered. I want you to
> come on Sunday, by yourself. Catch the 10.35 from
> Harringay Park, that gets you to Southend at 12.08.
> Come out of the railway station, walk straight across the
> road and along the road opposite. Walk along the
> left-hand side. I will see you. I am not giving my
> address in case you are followed. Just walk slowly
> along. If you come, will you bring me one size 15½ shirt
> and two collars, any colour will do. Also one pair of
> socks, dark ones, and a comb. I think that is all now.
> Best of luck – mine is gone …

The police asked Furnace's brother-in-law to go to
Southend as instructed, giving him the address to which
Furnace had been traced – 11 Whitegate Road. Superintendent Cornish of Scotland Yard and three other officers
shadowed him discreetly. As the brother-in-law walked
slowly along Whitegate Road, a curtain at the window of
number 11 twitched and Furnace looked out. He opened
the door to admit his relative, and the two men conversed

awkwardly until a few minutes later Superintendent
Cornish and his men entered the house via a rear door.
Thinking that Furnace was armed, they rushed and
overpowered him, but their belief proved groundless. He
had disposed of the weapon, probably before leaving
London.

In his statement, Furnace claimed that the shooting was
an accident. He said that in his office on the Monday
evening he was showing the young rent collector his
revolver as they were both interested in handguns. He
said that he kept it for protection. He claimed that he did
not know that it was loaded when he allowed Spatchett to
handle it, and it went off accidentally. This, of course, was
easily disproved, because if he had been showing a man a
gun and it had gone off, it would have hit him in the face,
or the chest or stomach, perhaps, but not with two shots
in the back!

Then came the usual plea, that he had found that
Spatchett was dead and panicked. How often do we find
that in the statements of those accused of murder! 'I
realized the position I was in, and lost my head ...' –
almost the very same words as those used by Norman
Thorne (*see* last chapter). 'I did not tell anyone I had shot
him,' the statement continued, 'and I thought the best
thing to do would be to destroy the body by setting fire to
my office. People would think the body was mine ...' It
was stretching the imagination a bit far to believe people
would think the body was his – Spatchett was twenty-five,
of slender build and 5ft. 9ins. tall, whereas Furnace was
forty-two, stockily-built and 6ft. And even if the rent
collector burned to a cinder, there were always the teeth.
Teeth just do not burn.

Asked how he had started the fire, Furnace described in
his statement that after sitting the body upright on the
office stool at the desk, he screwed up a quantity of
newspaper and set a candle in the middle of it. He then
sprinkled oil, turpentine and white spirit over it and lit the
candle, and beat a hasty retreat, pulling the door to and
locking it so as to delay entry by firemen for as long as
possible to give the fire a chance to gain a good foothold.
He threw the key into some weeds in a nearby back
garden, where it was later recovered by the police. He

took the leather bag containing the rent money which had been collected that day by his victim, which came to a total of £47 11s. 9d.

Furnace needed quite a bit of prompting by the police when he was making his statement. His recollection of various points seemed to be quite patchy; for example, he remembered accurately the sum of money he had taken, £47 11s. 9d. – the price of a man's life! – but he could not remember how or where he had disposed of the bag. 'I might have put it in someone's dustbin,' he told police. 'In London or Southend?' they asked. 'I cannot remember,' he said. The bag was never found.

Finally, the police read Furnace's statement over to him and asked him if he agreed with it and, if not, whether he wanted to make any amendments. He made some very minor ones, and then signed the statement and initialled the amendments. It was now ready to be produced in court at his trial, where he would be charged with murder.

No trial, however, would ever take place. Furnace, locked in his cell after making his statement, could be heard pacing back and forth. It was a very cold night and the overcoat he had been wearing for the journey from Southend to Kentish Town police station where he was taken after his arrest had been taken from him. He called for a guard and asked for his coat to be returned. This was done.

For some unknown reason, the overcoat was his one item of clothing that had not been searched; it had merely been hung on a peg in the room used for the depositing of prisoners' property. Furnace donned the coat and continued his restless pacing. Sleep was impossible. A guard looked through the spyhole in the cell door and asked him if he wanted a cup of tea; Furnace declined the offer.

Towards 7 a.m. the guard looked through the spyhole; the prisoner had stopped pacing about and all was very still. The prisoner appeared to be sleeping on the floor – a strange place to choose considering what a cold night it was. The floor was of concrete, whereas there was a bunk bed with two blankets in the cell. The guard decided to enter the cell and check in case the prisoner had been taken ill. It was discovered that he had swallowed the contents of a small phial of hydrochloric acid which he had secreted in his overcoat, sewn into the lining.

Twenty-four hours later, early on the morning of Tuesday, 18 January 1933, Samuel Furnace took his last breath in St Pancras's Hospital. In the mortuary of the same hospital lay the body of Walter Spatchett. It must be one of the very rare occasions in the history of crime that the body of the killer and the body of his victim lay in the same mortuary at the same time.

9

A Button was his Undoing

At eight p.m. on the night of Saturday, 9 February 1918, sixteen-year-old Nellie Trew (who was known to all as Peg) left home to go to the public library. She was an avid reader, and her room in her parents' modest home in Juno Terrace, Eltham, was full of second-hand books. Peg had a job as a junior clerk in the offices of Woolwich Arsenal and, while many of her contemporaries spent their spare cash on gramophone records, clothes and sweets, she preferred to search out bargains in the second-hand bookshops. She did not read trash – she preferred the well-loved classics such as Dickens, Scott, Jane Austen, Anna Sewell and R.D. Blackmore. Books she wanted to read but could not find second-hand, or could not afford to buy new, she borrowed from her local public library in Plumstead.

The library closed at 9 p.m. and her parents expected her back home by 9.30 at the latest. She was not the type to hang about with her friends in coffee-shops after the library closed. Besides, it was a raw night and pitch dark; it would be much warmer by the fire at home. So when ten p.m. came, then eleven, then midnight, her parents knew that something must have befallen her. It was just not like Peg to be late.

The following morning the police found her body on Eltham Common, about a quarter of a mile from her home. Her father had called them at midnight and they had started a search immediately, armed with torches. She lay under a clump of bushes, covered with mud as though she had been dragged to the spot – which indeed proved to be the case from drag marks extending about thirty yards. She had been savagely raped, but her knickers had been pulled on again afterwards in a hasty fashion. Beside her lay her handbag, which had not been interfered with, and her library book. She had been strangled manually.

As the police searched for clues, a careful examination of the scene of crime came up with an overcoat button which had not belonged to the dead girl. It had been threaded through only two of the four central holes with a piece of wire, not with the more usual cotton thread. One end of the wire ended in a sharp point, while the other was blunt. A badge also lay nearby in the grass; it was a replica of the badge of the Leicestershire Regiment.

The police deduced that both the button and the badge had been left at the scene by the assailant – the badge probably having worked loose from its pin during a struggle, and the button most likely having been pulled off by the victim as she fought with her attacker. The police surmised that the man was either a serving soldier or one recently discharged from the army, and they thought he was either a young single man who did not know how to sew on loose buttons with thread, or one who did not live with his family or have a landlady who would attend to such things as his mending.

The police arranged to have photographs of the button and the badge published in all the national daily papers, as well as the local ones. This soon produced results. A factory hand named Edward Farrell, who worked at the Hewson Manufacturing Company in Newman Street off Oxford Street, a firm of aeroplane component engineers, was enjoying the morning tea break when he spotted the photographs in his copy of the *Daily Mirror*. He immediately recognized the badge as one which a workmate of his named David Greenwood, a twenty-one-year-old turner, always wore in the lapel of his overcoat. Come to think of it, the button was similar to the buttons on his coat, too. But, he remembered, Dave hadn't been wearing the badge since last Saturday. He wondered what had happened to it, and decided to ask him.

Farrell spotted David Greenwood in the canteen during the afternoon tea break. He opened the paper and pointed to the photograph of the badge. 'That looks just like the badge you've been wearing,' he said. 'I see you've not been wearing it this week. What happened to it?'

Greenwood agreed that the badge in the photograph

looked like his badge, but did not say that it *was* his badge.
'I sold mine to a man in the pub last Saturday night,' he
said. 'Took a fancy to it. Offered me two bob. So I flogged
it to him for two shillings and went and bought a pint for
him and myself.'

'Don't you think you ought to go to the police?' Farrell
suggested.

'The police? – what for?'

'That chap who bought your badge – he might have
been the one who murdered that girl! Well, you never
know. Give the police a description of the man – it might
help them catch him.'

'Yes, I suppose I should,' Greenwood replied. 'OK, I'll
go and see them tonight.'

True to his word, David Greenwood went to Tottenham
Court Road police station after he finished work. He told
police his account of meeting a man in a pub who took a
fancy to his badge and bought it from him for two
shillings. 'Said he'd always wanted to be a soldier,' he
said, 'but when he tried to join the army they wouldn't
have him because his eyesight wasn't good enough. At
least that's what he told me – although he wasn't wearing
glasses.' Asked for a description, Greenwood said that his
drinking companion had been about the same age as
himself, thin-faced, an inch or two taller and wearing a
workman's cap, and said his name was Harry. He added
that the man had a Belfast accent.

The police took Greenwood's story with a large handful
of salt. They decided to make further inquiries into their
informant's background, and discovered that he had been
a near neighbour of Nellie Trew and probably knew her by
sight. Greenwood's bedsitter was in Jupiter Terrace, only a
street or two away from the dead girl's home.

Inspector Carlin of Scotland Yard, who was in charge of
the case, decided to interview Greenwood the following
day at Hewson's where he worked. Shown the badge,
Greenwood admitted that it was his. He was then asked to
clock off, fetch his coat and cap and accompany the
inspector to the Yard for further questioning.

In the squad car, the inspector noticed that all the
buttons were missing from the overcoat Greenwood was
wearing. 'I see you've lost all your coat buttons,' the

officer said. 'How long have they been off?'

'Oh, they've been off for a long time,' Greenwood replied. 'You know, I'm no good at this sewing lark. That's women's work!'

'Well, then – couldn't you have asked a lady friend to sew them back on for you?' Carlin asked.

'A lady friend? I haven't got a lady friend,' Greenwood said.

The inspector was taking a closer look at Greenwood's overcoat. He now spotted a tear in the fabric where one of the buttons had been. 'How did it get torn?' he asked.

'Must have caught on something and pulled out, I suppose,' the young man replied, his voice casual and seemingly unperturbed.

At police headquarters the button found beside Nellie Trew's body was produced, and found to have a small piece of fabric adhering to the back which exactly matched the tear in the overcoat. It was also found that the wire Greenwood had used to re-attach the button to the coat had originally formed part of a spring of a type manufactured by Hewson's.

David Greenwood was formally arrested and charged with the murder of Nellie Trew. When charged, he replied, 'It wasn't me.' He was sent for trial at the Old Bailey.

At his trial before Mr Justice Atkin, which opened on 24 April 1918, Greenwood pleaded not guilty. Sir Travers Humphreys prosecuted, and Greenwood was defended by Mr Slesser.

In his defence, Greenwood stated that the overcoat was part of his demob issue on being discharged on medical grounds from the RAMC in 1917. He had never liked the coat, he said, and claimed that he had not been wearing it on the night of 9 February.

Mr Slesser pointed out the excellent service record of the accused. He had enlisted as soon as the war started and had taken part in the fighting at Ypres, where he had been buried alive by the earth thrown up by an exploding shell. Subsequently he had been invalided out with shellshock, neurasthenia and a heart condition. Mr Slesser challenged Sir Bernard Spilsbury to admit that his client's physical condition was such that he would not have had the strength to overpower a healthy, well-built teenage girl. Sir Bernard could not see his way clear to committing himself either way.

The prosecution made much of the fact that Greenwood was shy and awkward where women were concerned and could not make normal social relationships. This, they contended, made him more liable to give vent to his frustrations by raping women. To this the defence replied that the defendant was accused of raping only *one* woman. The prosecution argued that it was the only one known about ... but it was their contention that the murder had been a premeditated act, even if the rape had not. Once the accused had given way to the impulse to rape, the prosecution averred, he knew that he would have to silence his victim if he were to escape the consequences of his act. Therefore he killed his victim afterwards in the full knowledge of what he was doing. Credence was given to the theory that Greenwood had known his victim, albeit slightly, by this need to prevent her from reporting him to the police as the man who had raped her.

The jury took three hours to weigh all the evidence, finding him guilty by a unanimous verdict. They added a recommendation to mercy on account of his youth, his good character as a soldier and his services to his country. When asked if he had anything to say before sentence was passed, he repeated that he was innocent of the charges brought against him. The judge then sentenced him to death.

He appealed, and on the very eve of his execution which had been set for 31 May 1918, he was reprieved. His sentence was commuted to penal servitude for life. For some considerable time various people and organizations campaigned for his release, but it was fifteen years before this took place, in 1933, when he was thirty-six.

10
Murder Without a Body

The war was over and, for those Polish soldiers who had remained in Britain after hostilities had ceased, the time had come to make the decision as to what career to pursue after leaving the army. One of them, fifty-eight-year-old Michał Onufrejczyk, had always dreamed of owning his own farm, although he had no farming experience. He had been a warrant officer, which is about as far from agriculture as one can get. Undeterred, he scanned the advertisements for a suitable farm in the local newspapers of South Wales where he was living after the war ended, and spotted the details of a farm called Cefn Hendre, about half a mile from the village of Cwmdu in Carmarthenshire. The farm was cheap because it was in near-derelict condition with ramshackle buildings and poor, stony soil. He obtained a loan from Polish Army Resettlement Corps funds, and moved in.

Michał Onufrejczyk soon found that the farm was far more than he could manage single-handed, and decided to advertise for a partner. Eventually, from the various applicants who came along for an interview, he chose Stanislaw Sykut, who was the same age as himself and who had been working as a male nurse in a hospital in Shropshire after his discharge from the army. Sykut was a quiet, unassuming individual, while Onufrejczyk had a violent temper, and would flare up at almost nothing. Considering that he spoke very little English and no Welsh, and many of his neighbours were Welsh-speaking only, it is little wonder that Onufrejczyk was a taciturn, even surly fellow. This ill-assorted couple entered into a partnership to run the farm jointly for a consideration of £600, the half-share handed over by Sykut to Onufrejczyk,

and the legal documents were signed by the partners on
10 April 1953.

Onufrejczyk had been a good soldier – he had nine
campaign medals to prove it – but he was a poor farmer
and left most of the hard work involved to his new partner
who, not unnaturally, took rather a dim view of the
situation, and the two had words on a number of
occasions. When forming the partnership Onufrejczyk
had made the proposition sound attractive enough, and
the partnership deeds stipulated that the work was to be
done equally by both of them as well as the profits being
shared equally between them. But it was undoubtedly the
payment of the £600 that had been Onufrejczyk's main
motivation in forming the partnership; the farm had been
losing money and he was getting deeper and deeper into
debt.

The reserved Welsh valley folk who were the
neighbours of the two farmers of Cefn Hendre wondered
how long this uneasy partnership would last, as they
waited and watched for signs of gradual improvement in
the run-down condition of the place. Every day they saw
Sykut hard at work in the fields, Onufrejczyk too
sometimes, and on the days when both were outside they
were rarely observed to be talking. Onufrejczyk was not
the kind of man to lean on his hoe and chat. In fact it
seemed rather as though the two partners took some pains
to avoid each other.

Stanislaw Sykut toiled unremittingly for several months
in the uncomfortably strained silence that did duty for the
company of Michal Onufrejczyk, until one day he decided
that enough was enough. On this day, one of the
grudgingly given days off that he was allowed, he made a
trip to the office of a local solicitor, unbeknown to his
partner, instructing him to draw up and prepare the
requisite six months' notice of termination of the
partnership on 14 November. He realized grimly, as he
returned to the farm, that he would be very unpopular
with his partner when he received the notice from the
solicitor …

In his letter, the solicitor informed Onufrejczyk that
unless Onufrejczyk or someone else on his behalf paid
Sykut his share in full – in other words, repay his

investment plus added profits – the farm would be put up to auction. Onufrejczyk was, to put it mildly, not a little put out on receiving this communication, and the two men were at loggerheads. How could Onufrejczyk raise such a sum? All his money had gone into clearing his debts and purchasing farm stock from which he hoped to realize a profit in due time. November 14 came and went; Onufrejczyk ignored it. It would to him be just a day like any other. Life at Cefn Hendre must have been pretty intolerable with the two men at 'daggers drawn'. But Sykut continued to live at the farm.

On 14 December he took a horse to the village blacksmith to be shod. The blacksmith tried to draw him into conversation, but his efforts were unsuccessful. Sykut had arranged, after returning the horse to the farm, to meet a friend, a fellow Pole named Józef Bryda, in Llandilo, that same afternoon. The two friends agreed to meet again in Llandilo on 16 December when Sykut had an appointment for an interview for a job he wanted to take up on leaving the farm. Bryda was to accompany him to act as interpreter. To Bryda's astonishment, Sykut failed to turn up for the appointment.

Bryda, remembering how keen Sykut had been to get the job, was convinced that his friend had met with some illness or accident which had prevented him from keeping his appointment, and decided to call at Cefn Hendre to find out what had happened. He was greeted by Onufrejczyk in one of his usual surly moods, who did not let him into the house, and told him shortly that Sykut had gone into Llandilo to see his doctor.

Bryda was not satisfied. Llandilo is not a very big town and, since the doctor's surgery was only a few doors from his (Bryda's) own house, it is highly unlikely that he would have missed him, either in the street or at the bus stop, going into or leaving town. Sykut would have been driving Onufrejczyk's battered old black car, easily recognizable by three old dents in the offside bumper where at some time it had received a hefty bash. Bryda had not seen the car. Furthermore, since Bryda and Sykut were old friends from army days, it is more than likely that Sykut would have dropped in to pay him a short visit after leaving the doctor's.

Bryda, who had lived in Llandilo for many years, had a friend, a Welshman, who was a sheriff's officer. He decided to go and see him and report his growing suspicion that Sykut was apparently missing. He was not the kind of man who would just fail to turn up for a job interview with no subsequent explanation to anybody, and he frankly did not believe Onufrejczyk when he had told him that his friend had gone to the doctor's. There was something not quite right somewhere, he told the officer. Just a gut feeling, maybe, but still *something*. He asked the officer to visit the farm and see what he could find out.

The Sheriff's Officer, accompanied by a Polish court interpreter, went to Cefn Hendre to see Onufrejczyk. It was a bitter December day, but Onufrejczyk refused to allow the two men past the front door and insisted that they talk in the yard as a fierce wind gusted down from the surrounding hills. Snow was not far away as the three men spoke in the teeth of the gale. The Sheriff's Officer informed Onufrejczyk that he was making a routine inquiry about Stanisław Sykut on behalf of his friend Józef Bryda, who was concerned that he had neither kept an appointment he had nor been in touch with him since. Was he ill? Had he had an accident with farm machinery? Onufrejczyk told them that Sykut had gone to London for a fortnight on business, and that it was his own private business and no concern of the Sheriff's Officer or anyone else. He then slammed the door on his visitors.

'Charming fellow,' observed the interpreter.

By this time gossip was rife in the village of Cwmdu. At the post office Sykut's mail lay uncollected, and his Post Office Savings' Bank account had not been added to for weeks – he had usually managed to deposit a small sum each week. The Llandilo solicitor, too, had received no replies to his letters regarding the proposed termination of the partnership. When it was discovered that his ration book had been left with the village grocer for several weeks and had not been collected, Bryda and the Sheriff's Officer decided that the police should be informed and Sykut declared to be officially missing in mysterious circumstances. He had not told anyone at all of any intention to leave the area; if he had done so, he would not have left behind his ration book or his mail. It was confirmed that he had never visited his doctor on 14 December as Onufrejczyk had stated.

Mr T.H. Lewis, the chief constable of the combined police force of Carmarthenshire and Cardiganshire, was confident that some harm had befallen Stanisław Sykut, and he had no difficulty in persuading a magistrate to issue a search warrant for Cefn Hendre Farm. The chief constable himself led a team of detectives to the farm and carried out a systematic search of the farmhouse, outbuildings and land, while Onufrejczyk stood by fuming with fury. Eventually, realizing that his truculent remarks would get him nowhere, he shuffled off into the fields with his dog.

About thirty acres of Cefn Hendre Farm were boggy, and police dogs were brought in to search this part of the land. Nothing was found. In the house, no trace of the missing Pole could be found, except his shaving tackle. It would have been unlikely that Sykut had left home without his shaving gear as he was never known to have worn a beard, or even a moustache.

The last person to have seen Sykut alive was the blacksmith, who had shod the horse on 14 December and entered the date in his book. He was positive that the last he saw of him was walking up the steep track to the farm with the horse. He had never seen him since. His house adjoined his forge and workshop so that he had an unobstructed view of the track to the farm at all times. He was seldom away from home and could not have failed to see or hear any car or other vehicle making its laborious way to or from Cefn Hendre Farm.

The blacksmith was to be an important witness later. On one occasion, he said, Onufrejczyk called on him asking to see his day-book in which he had written the date on which his horse had been shod, and was shown the entry for 14 December. Onufrejczyk insisted that it had been on the 17th, and when he unsuccessfully tried to persuade the blacksmith to change the entry from the 14th to the 17th, he became extremely abusive and was still shouting as he returned up the hillside track, having failed in his attempt.

In the meantime, Onufrejczyk was trapping himself

more and more inextricably in the web of deceit and lies
he had woven. Forged documents purporting to bear
Sykut's signature were discovered, and a man was found
who had been bribed by Onufrejczyk to impersonate
Sykut to sign a document when a solicitor had insisted
that Sykut attend personally at his office, having informed
Onufrejczyk that the signed documents he possessed
were insufficient to give him a clear title to the farm. When
confronted with these allegations, Onufrejczyk tried to
bluff his way out.

With the circumstantial evidence piling up, on the
advice of two senior members of Scotland Yard's police
force a further and more intensive search of Cefn Hendre
Farm was carried out, this time by a much larger
task-force, including the Director of the South Wales and
Monmouthshire Forensic Science Laboratory and his staff,
as well as a large body of police-officers.

Although clean and habitable, the farmhouse was in a
poor state of repair. The floor was tiled and cemented, but
no disturbance was evident. The low-beamed ceiling and
the walls were next to come under the close scrutiny of the
experts. Their patience was rewarded when they found
more than two thousand tiny stains – splash spots – on
three of the four walls of the kitchen as well as on the
ceiling and the walls of the passage leading out to the
farmyard. A dark stain was also found on a Welsh dresser
in the kitchen, about the size and shape of a stain which
could have been made by a bloody hand being rested
upon it. Two minute fragments of bone were also found
near the fireplace in the kitchen. The scientists confirmed
that all the bloodstains were human.

On 12 March Onufrejczyk, asked for an explanation of
the stains found in his kitchen, trotted out the excuse that
he had been butchering rabbits. Knowing that their
suspect was lying, the investigators decided to leave him
to stew and to return and interview him again a few days
later. This they did on 23 March. This time Onufrejczyk
'suddenly remembered' that Sykut had cut his hand on a
mowing machine and that he had seen him standing by
the dresser waving his hand about while his partner had
gone to fetch the first aid box, and that blood had sprayed
round the walls of the kitchen. 'If you believe that story,'

one police officer said, 'you'll believe that there are fairies at the bottom of your garden. Even a complete moron would know that waving your hand about would make it bleed more, not stop the bleeding!'

No body, however, could be found, and the case against Onufrejczyk, built as it was on circumstantial evidence, was far from complete. Extensive inquiries were made throughout Britain to try to ascertain whether Sykut was indeed alive in some other part of the country, and even European authorities were consulted to find out whether Sykut had decided to return to Poland, although this was felt to be very unlikely. Even Interpol could not trace him. No one could turn up a single person who had seen Stanisław Sykut after 14 December 1954.

On 19 August 1955 the decision was taken to charge Onufrejczyk with the murder of his partner. He was driven in a police car the fifteen miles from Cefn Hendre Farm to Carmarthen. After his remand, he then found himself in Swansea Prison to await trial at Glamorgan Assizes.

Mr W.L. Mars-Jones, on behalf of the Director of Public Prosecutions, called evidence to show that the motive for the murder of Stanisław Sykut was his fear of being dispossessed of the farm, and the avoidance of repaying his partner on the termination of their agreement. This implied a high degree of premeditation, since the accused had first tried other methods such as the forging of documents and the deception of a solicitor, without having been able to secure his future by these dubious means.

The trial, before Mr Justice Oliver, took twelve days, and seventy witnesses were called for the prosecution. In his summing-up, the judge pointed out to the jury that murder can be proved, in certain cases, by circumstantial evidence, notwithstanding that no body is ever found and that the accused has made no confession to any participation in the crime. 'The circumstantial evidence,' he continued, 'should be so cogent and compelling as to convince a jury that upon no rational hypothesis other than murder can the facts [of death] be discounted.'

The jury was indeed satisfied that enough evidence had been produced to prove beyond all reasonable doubt that the victim had been murdered by the accused, despite the absence of his body. They were out for just under three hours before returning a verdict of guilty. The judge then donned the black cap and sentenced Onufrejczyk to death.

The main ground of his appeal was that no body had ever been found, but this carried little weight with the Court of Criminal Appeal, who dismissed the application on 11 January 1955. In their ruling the Appeal Court judges agreed with Mr Justice Oliver that the fact of death, like any other fact, can be proved by circumstantial evidence. However, Onufrejczyk and his solicitors were not satisfied and applied for leave to appeal to the House of Lords, but this was refused by the Attorney-General. On 24 January Onufrejczyk was reprieved, and the death sentence commuted to life imprisonment.

Onufrejczyk served only ten years before being released in 1965. To the great amazement of everyone concerned, the very first thing he did on his release was to return to Llandilo, where he made exhaustive inquiries as to whether anyone had seen Sykut during his sojourn in jail. He also visited a local solicitor to collect the war medals, his pride and joy, which had been kept in the lawyer's safe while he was in prison.

The following year Onufrejczyk moved to Yorkshire and settled in Bradford, where he hoped to begin a new life, but although he had successfully cheated the hangman he was killed in a road traffic accident the same year.

The body of Stanislaw Sykut has never been found. Theories abound as to how he met his grisly end. It seems most likely that his body was dismembered and distributed in the bog which covered a large part of the farm. There, the pieces would have sunk without trace. Local superstition has it that the bog is bottomless.

11
One Man's Private War

Young men were disappearing and turning up later – dead – at an alarming rate in California. Not only were the police perplexed but the military authorities, too, were very perturbed, because more than three-quarters of the victims were marines. Was there someone out there who had a grievance against marines?

It all started in December 1972, when the body of a twenty-year-old marine named Edward Daniel Moore, based at Camp Pendleton, was found in the Seal Beach area. He had been sexually assaulted and strangled, and traces of drugs were found in his body. Since he was not a drug-user, it was assumed that he had been drugged prior to the assault and murder. And, while no further victims were to surface in the years immediately following, it was to set the pattern for a terrifying series of sixteen known murders in the years to come – possibly a good many more.

On 26 March 1975 Keith Crotwell, nineteen, a resident of Long Beach, disappeared in mysterious circumstances. He was last seen alive in a Long Beach car-park where he had told friends he was going to buy some pot from a man he had met earlier that day. A few days later his head was found in the sea by two fishermen, and his skeleton was discovered seven months later in the Laguna Hills outside Los Angeles.

The following month a nineteen-year-old student named Ronnie Eugene Wiebe was found dead at the entrance to the San Diego freeway; it appeared that he had been drugged and thrown from a car. Because he had not been subjected to any apparent sexual violence his death was not at that time linked to the other two.

On 11 June the body of Ronald Gerald Young, aged twenty-three, was found only hours after he had been released from the Orange County jail for a drunk and disorderly offence. He had been stabbed four times through the heart and castrated.

1976 opened with the disappearance of a young man on New Year's Day in San Juan Capistrano, a town about half way between the El Toro Marine Air Base and Camp Pendleton, where the first victim had been stationed. Mark Hall, who was twenty-two years of age and was not a marine but worked in electronics, had been living in a motel in Santa Ana. A native of Idaho, he had attended a party in San Juan Capistrano, which he had left at 4 a.m. saying he was going home. He was never seen alive again. A few days later his body was found beside the freeway. He had been strangled and castrated.

Police were quick to link four 1978 murders with the unknown killer who chose only young men as his victims. In April Scott Hughes, a marine, was found strangled beside a freeway, while in June Roland Young was found dead in Irvine, and a marine named Richard Allen Keith, from Camp Pendleton, who was twenty, was found naked and strangled in the Laguna Hills on 18 June. He had last been seen alive in the town of Carson by a friend. The following month Keith Arthur Klingbell, thirty-two, of Everett in the State of Washington, a transient carnival worker, was found beside the San Diego freeway on 6 July. He had choked to death on his own vomit. Klingbell was much older than any of the other victims, but looked younger than his years. Because of the disparity in age-group some police officers did not at first link his death with the other victims, but the pattern of the killings fitted too closely to enable them to rule out the connection.

Two marines were found dead in 1980, after which there was a hiatus of three years, during which time police and public alike were wondering whether the murders had stopped. The killer, they theorized, could have left the state, or be in jail for some unrelated offence, or even have died. Only some physical cause could be preventing him from continuing his grisly handiwork, for as the police well knew, the compulsive serial murderer does not voluntarily cease killing. In fact, the intervals between the murders, given no external inhibiting factor, tend to decrease with time.

It came, therefore, as no surprise when on 27 January 1983 Eric Church, aged twenty-one, of Hartford, Connecticut, a marine serving at the El Toro base, was found dead beside the San Diego freeway, to be followed on 13 February by the finding of the emasculated and strangled bodies of two other marines, Geoffrey Nelson, aged eighteen and Roger de Vaul, who was twenty. Both had been based at Camp Pendleton and had failed to return to base after being seen together on 12 February hitch-hiking towards San Diego.

It was in this same area that on 14 May, two California Highway Patrol officers, Sergeant Mike Howard and Patrolman Mike Sterling, were cruising at about 1.15 a.m. They had shortly before this arrested a drunk-driver on the eight-lane stretch of the interstate road between San Diego and Los Angeles, and were feeling very pleased with themselves, when they noticed a Toyota some way ahead weaving erratically about and edging towards the offside in a manner hazardous to other traffic.

'Oh, no – not another one!' breathed Howard. He paced the Toyota for about a mile until they reached the approach to a pull-off point, when he activated his flashing light and siren, signalling the Toyota to pull off the highway and stop. The driver of the Toyota did so, but instead of remaining in his car as most drivers do in similar circumstances, he slid out from behind the wheel and walked briskly towards the police car.

'This guy must have something in the car he doesn't want us to see,' observed Sterling.

'Drugs, most likely,' Howard replied. 'Or maybe stolen goods. I'd say dope, though, more likely.'

Sterling told the man to face the patrol car and put his hands up on the roof while he frisked him. He found no weapons or drugs. He then administered the standard breathalyser test, which proved negative. In the meantime, Howard went over to the Toyota. Another man was sitting in the passenger seat. 'Come on!' Howard said. 'Out!' The man in the passenger seat did not budge. 'I said, get out of the car,' Howard ordered. The man did not reply and continued to sit in the car without moving.

Exasperated, Howard switched on his torch. It was then that he realized that the man would never get out of the car. He was dead. He was young and dressed in marine uniform, the trousers at half-mast exposing his genitals, but Howard could see no blood or other signs of violence.

Howard returned to the patrol car and handcuffed the driver of the Toyota.

'Hey, what's he done?' Sterling asked. 'He's not drunk. No drugs or weapons on him.'

'Go over and look at his car!' was the reply.

'My God!' Sterling exclaimed as he returned to his partner. 'It looks like we've got him at last!' He wiped perspiration from his brow. 'Let's see who these guys are.' On checking their identities, the driver of the Toyota turned out to be a Long Beach resident named Randolph Kraft, a thirty-eight-year-old computer programmer, while his dead companion was a twenty-five-year-old marine named Terry Lee Gambrel, based at El Toro, but originally from the tiny village of Crothersville in Indiana, where he had grown up on his father's farm. But he had, it was later found, always wanted to see the world, so he had joined the marines. A strapping six-footer, he had seen some European countries after a posting to Germany, but had never made it to the Far East – his motivating dream. He had last been seen alive by his twin brother when he was home on leave before hitch-hiking back to his base in California. But before he ever reached his base, he encountered the man who was conducting, it seemed, a one-man war on gays.

Kraft, in custody, admitted that he saw Gambrel hitch-hiking and offered him a lift to El Toro, but he refused to make any comment on the fact that his companion had been found dead in his car or that he had interfered with him in any way.

Yet, during the subsequent investigations, it was surmised that not all the victims were gay. Most of the bodies contained varying amounts of stupefying drugs – the kind that would tend to knock a person out quickly and render him incapable of resisting whatever advances might be made to him. Ativan, a depressant of this type, was found in Gambrel's body. It was not known how these drugs were administered but it was thought they could have been slipped into glasses of liquor or even sandwiches or hamburgers. Bottles of liquor, glasses and an empty lunch-box which showed signs of having contained food, were all found in Kraft's car, and alcohol was found in the blood of several of the victims, including Gambrel.

It would seem that Kraft, himself gay, was so utterly appalled by the knowledge of his own homosexuality that he was under a psychological compulsion to blot out the revulsion and self-loathing he felt for his deeds by destroying his victims afterwards. Furthermore, in more than half of the cases he had amputated their genitals – which in psychological terms may have been a symbolic act destroying their male status and rendering them 'women' – thus rationalizing his sex drive as 'normal'.

Once it was verified that, as a freelance computer programmer working out of his own home, Kraft travelled extensively throughout the United States, police nation-wide were asked to search their files for unsolved crimes matching the *modus operandi* of the ones being investigated in California. The pattern, in the main, seemed mostly to be strangulation and mutilation after sexual assault, the use of drugs and/or liquor, and the subsequent discarding of the body from a car alongside one of the highways that traversed the country. A Michigan police chief reported that he and his men had been investigating the death of two young cousins whose bodies had been buried near a water storage tower in Grand Rapids; it was discovered that Kraft and the cousins had been staying in the same hotel at the same time. In Oregon, officers had more than a dozen unsolved homosexual murders on their books, some dating back to 1972, when it was thought that the series of killings had started. Various circumstances linking Kraft to these Oregon cases were discovered; in one case Kraft had attended a computer programming evening class which had also been attended by one of the victims; in another, both had stayed at the same hotel on the same dates. Other cases surfaced placing Kraft in Ohio, Washington State and New York State at times when similar murders took place. What amazed investigators was the facility with which Kraft had thrown dead bodies from his car on to the sides of heavily-travelled main highways without being seen. Even if this was always done during the hours of darkness – as in the case of Gambrel – traffic could still be, and often was, heavy on these main arterial roads at night.

Kraft was arraigned in August 1983 for the six counts of murder in Orange County, California, and the final court hearing was scheduled for late September, by which time a further ten counts of murder were added to the charges, plus nine counts of sexual mutilation and three counts of sodomy – these were specimen charges.

Testimony from Deputy District Attorney Brian Brown included evidence that a number of photographs had been found both at the accused's home and under the floorboards of his Toyota car, in which a number of the victims were shown dead. One was shown seated in the car in the same way that Gambrel had been found, in the passenger seat and with lowered trousers. A prescription container of the drug Ativan was also found hidden in the car.

A vital witness had been found and persuaded to come forward at the trial. His testimony would go far to prove that Kraft had drugged and attacked victims in his own home in at least some of the cases. Lance Pardee, twenty-six, now living in Colorado but at the material time a Long Beach resident, testified that in 1970, when he was thirteen, he met Kraft near the Huntington Beach pier and got into conversation with him. After chatting for a while, he said, Kraft invited him to his Long Beach home. Once there, he said, Kraft gave him eight pills and a joint (marijuana cigarette), as a result of which he immediately became drowsy and felt very weak. Kraft forced him to perform oral sex, following which he sodomized him on two occasions. Before allowing him to leave, he continued, Kraft forced him to say that he would not tell anyone what had happened.

Pardee said that he put on his clothes and stumbled out into the street, and people who saw him called an ambulance. In hospital he told doctors he had been drugged, but did not mention the rape, and it seemed that no one thought to examine him. He refused to name or describe the person who had given him the drugs. When the prosecutor asked him why he did not summon the courage to tell someone about the incident, he replied, 'I was only thirteen! I was scared to hell!' Only after thirteen years, with his attacker safely in custody, did he find the necessary courage.

Another piece of evidence produced by the prosecution was a document found in Kraft's car giving cryptic notes which were obviously references to persons, places and dates and which, on analysis, were found to tie in with many of the known crimes: for example, 'Two in one day 13 Feb.' referred to Roger de Vaul and Geoffrey Nelson, both killed on that date; 'New Year's' referred to Mark Hall; 'Parking Lot 26 March' referred to Keith Crotwell, last seen alive on that date in a car-park; and so on. The documentation of their crimes in this way seems to be quite a commonly-encountered feature of many multiple murderers, and would appear to be yet another facet of the macabre compulsions that hold them in their thrall.

A further compulsion many serial killers have is to keep as macabre 'souvenirs' articles belonging to their victims. An electric shaver belonging to Eric Church was found in Kraft's home, as well as a silver cigarette-lighter which had belonged to another marine. It was also proved that this latter victim had been killed in Kraft's Long Beach home on account of rug fibres found on the body matching rug fibres found in the house.

Kraft never admitted to any of the killings at any time. In addition to the sixteen counts of murder and twelve other specimen charges, he is suspected of at least another twelve unsolved murders in California, twelve in Oregon and two in Michigan, as well as three in other states. These cases are all the subject of further investigation as at the time of writing, and Randolph Kraft is still in the Orange County jail awaiting the outcome of these investigations. Sentence was deferred on the charges to which he answered at his trial in September 1983 until such time as these out-of-state inquiries could be finalized. In the meantime, it is possible that this man could face a total of forty-five murder charges in due course of time. But one thing is certain: whether five or forty-five, Randolph Kraft will never be allowed to go free on America's highways again.

12
The Mask of Death

Hitler's bombs were no respecters of persons, or places. A hospital or a church was just as likely to be demolished as a military target, and in fact many of the so-called 'doodlebugs' that landed in London during the blitz fell wide of the mark. By no stretch of the imagination could a Baptist chapel be considered a military target.

The place of worship in Vauxhall Road, Kennington, South London, had been all but flattened by one of these 'doodlebugs', and in due time a gang of workmen was sent to complete the demolition and prepare the site for redevelopment after the war. In the meantime, the structure was unsafe and had to be rendered less of a hazard to the public.

John Parslow was one of the workmen engaged on the task. In the rubble-strewn cellar of the chapel he spotted a heavy stone slab set in the floor, looking rather like a gravestone. He prised this up with his pick, and was not really very surprised to see a skeleton beneath the slab. Just another victim of the blitz, he thought to himself as he slid his shovel underneath the skeleton and lifted it clear. The head remained in the grave. He told his foreman what he had found, and it was decided that the police ought to be informed so that the remains could if possible be identified. Many people had gone missing during bombings and the police were always being asked to look for them. They had lists of missing persons, presumed killed by bombs, with descriptions for checking if any bodies turned up during just such demolition works.

Detective Inspectors Hatton and Keeling were called in to investigate the find, and after the preliminary site examination and photography the bones were wrapped in brown paper packages and taken to the mortuary in

Southwark, where they were examined by Professor Keith Simpson, the Home Office pathologist. In the abdominal cavity there was a womb, which established that the victim was female; some soft tissues still clung to the bones in places, thus ruling out a long-time burial. The body could have lain there not more than a year to eighteen months, but the chapel had been bombed two years before, in August 1940. It was now 17 July 1942; thus, the pathologist reasoned, the remains were not those of a blitz victim. Death had occurred *after* the bomb had dropped.

At the inquest Simpson asked the coroner for permission to remove the remains to his pathology laboratory at Guy's Hospital for a more detailed examination. He found that the head had not become detached from the skeleton when the workman had lifted it on his shovel; it had been cut off after death. Both arms had been dismembered at the elbow-joints, and both legs at the knees. There were some blackened areas on the skull and the legs caused by fire. The case looked very much like murder – it was certainly not a case of damage by bomb blast.

Some pieces of the skeleton were missing, mostly from the limbs, and the pathologist spent two afternoons with the police team who were sifting almost three tons of rubble and earth under the floor of the chapel cellar, but no bones, or portions of bones, came to light. Simpson noted some yellowish powder on the earth where the body had been buried, traces of which also adhered to the head and neck of the corpse. There was also a wooden chest found near the site of the grave, just under five feet in length.

John Ryffel, the Home Office analyst and head of the Department of Clinical Chemistry at Guy's Hospital, analysed the yellow powder found in the grave and on the body, and pronounced this to be slaked lime. The person who had dismembered and buried the body evidently had no chemical knowledge, and this was to prove his undoing and incidentally assist the forensic scientists and the police. Lime has a reputation for destroying human flesh and the odours of decomposition; but *slaked* lime works in just the opposite way: it acts as a preservative, destroying the maggots, beetles and other agents which hasten the decomposition of a dead body. In this case, the area of the throat had been preserved to a remarkable degree, and an injury was apparent which proved that strangulation had occurred. The upper horn of the thyroid cartilage on the right side of the larynx (voice-box) had been fractured; a blood clot had formed at this point. This proved that John Parslow could not have damaged it when digging up the skeleton; it had been broken while the victim was alive.

This particular bone, it can be said authoritatively, is never broken except by pressure from a strangler's grip. Professor Simpson was emphatic on this point. 'This bone can be broken in no other way,' he said, 'and I am quite prepared to say so in court. This woman was strangled.'

They had the cause of death; now they must try to find out the victim's identity. The body was reassembled and measured, and the woman's height was estimated at 5ft. ½in. It was a simple matter to calculate her approximate age by an examination of the various component plates of the skull, which join together at certain stages in growth and development. The lower parts were completely fused, while the upper ones had fusion still in progress, and there was no fusion between the two groups. That put her age at between forty and fifty.

A small fragment of hair still remained attached to the skull; it was dark brown, going grey. The womb was enlarged, and an X-ray was taken to ascertain whether the woman had been pregnant, but the enlargement turned out to be a fibroid about four inches in diameter. If the woman had been pregnant, foetal bones would have shown on the X-ray.

The teeth were the next item to come under close scrutiny. The lower jaw was missing, but the upper jaw contained enough dental work to clinch identification if only the dentist who had carried out the work could be located. Two of the right molars had been filled, as also had the first left molar. Marks were found which had been made by the metal clamp of a dental plate. The palate was abnormally high, and there was considerable thickening of a bone in the region of the posterior teeth. 'Find the dentist who carried out this work,' Simpson told police, 'and you'll have an identification. It's as good as a portrait.'

Inspector Keeling had been meanwhile working through the lists of missing persons, and he discovered that Rachel Dobkin, the wife of Harry Dobkin, who was the firewatcher at the Baptist Chapel before it was bombed, had disappeared after setting out to collect arrears of maintenance from him about fifteen months previously. She had been separated from her husband for more than twenty years. Rachel's sister Polly had reported her disappearance to the police.

The police interviewed Polly, who informed them that her sister was forty-seven and about 5ft. 1in. tall. 'She had dark brown hair going grey,' she said, 'and she had been going to hospital for some kind of internal complaint – a fibroid tumour, I think.'

'Do you know who her dentist was?' she was asked.

'Oh, yes – the same one I have. Barnett Kopkin, in Stoke Newington.' Polly also gave the police a photograph of Rachel.

Dr Marie Watson, of the Mildmay Mission Hospital in Bethnal Green, confirmed that she had examined Mrs Rachel Dobkin in October 1939 and found a fibroid growth in the uterus. Another doctor confirmed her findings and suggested an operation, which Mrs Dobkin had refused.

Inspector Keeling's next call was at the offices of Barnett Kopkin, the Stoke Newington dentist. He immediately recognized Rachel Dobkin from the photograph and told the inspector that she had been his patient for six years from April 1934 to March 1940. He was asked to attend at the forensic laboratory at Guy's Hospital where Professor Keith Simpson was waiting to show him the upper jaw of the victim. Kopkin did not even stop to be formally introduced. 'That's my patient!' he burst out excitedly. 'That's Mrs Dobkin! Those are my fillings!' And in that dramatic moment the identity of the Baptist Chapel victim was confirmed beyond all doubt.

Professor Simpson now decided to superimpose the full-face photograph he had of the dead woman upon the X-ray photograph of her skull. The dead woman's portrait was enlarged to the same size as the X-ray photograph. Fresh photographs were then developed on X-ray film, a negative of the skull and a positive of the portrait, and the two were then superimposed. Not a single dissimilarity was found; the portrait fitted the skull like a mask – the mask of death.

Now that the identification was certain, it only remained to find the murderer. But it was for the police, not Professor Simpson, to show who had killed Rachel Dobkin.

In 1923 Mrs Dobkin had obtained a maintenance order against her husband, who had failed to maintain her or their child. Harry Dobkin was most irregular with his payments, and served several terms of imprisonment for default. Rachel, in desperation, resorted to the expedient of waylaying him in the street to demand the payments to which she was entitled, and he had come to regard her as a nuisance who pestered him at all hours. In fact on four occasions he struck her and she summoned him for assault.

On 11 April 1941 – it was Good Friday – the couple had tea together in a café in Dalston. They left at about 6.30 p.m., and Rachel was never seen again. Polly reported her disappearance to the police, saying she suspected Harry of foul play. But England was at war, and the police had more than enough to deal with, undermanned and overworked as they were, to deal with the matter.

On the night of 14 April 1941 a mysterious fire occurred at the Baptist Chapel. It was mysterious because there had been no enemy action that night, and no inflammable materials were kept on the premises. Harry Dobkin was the official firewatcher for the building, but he raised no alarm – a fact that was mysterious in itself. In fact the fire was first noticed by a policeman on the beat at 3.20 a.m. He called the fire brigade and went into the chapel, where he met Harry Dobkin. 'I thought you were the official firewatcher here,' a fireman said. 'Why didn't you call us?'

'I thought I would try to put it out myself,' Dobkin replied, 'and not bother you chaps. You have enough on your plate already, what with all these incendiary bombs the Jerries are sending us.'

The fire was put out and the minister, the Rev. Herbert Burgess, was sent for to come and take stock of the damage. In the cellar he saw the charred remains of a straw-filled mattress, which appeared to have been ripped open and straw scattered in small heaps on the floor. Mr Burgess asked Dobkin if he knew how the fire had started, and he replied in the negative. The minister felt very strongly that Dobkin knew more than he was telling, and that the fire had been deliberately started, but he kept his opinions to himself, apart from writing his thoughts on the subject in a notebook.

The next day, 16 April, a bomb fell less than 250 yards from the chapel, killing twenty-three and injuring fifty. The bomb was in fact a land mine, and, as may well be imagined, such a disaster would have occupied the attention of police and other authorities to the extent of crowding out the report of a small localized fire which had been quickly put out and as quickly forgotten. Finally, in May, the police asked Harry Dobkin when he had last seen his wife, to which he replied that it had been 11 April at the Dalston teashop. Rachel's photograph was published, along with the photographs of other missing persons, in the *Police Gazette*, and the report was then filed. Out of sight, out of mind, it seemed.

It was more than a year later when a beat constable, passing the Baptist Chapel, saw lights shining from an upstairs window, in contravention of the wartime blackout regulations, and went in to investigate. There he encountered Harry Dobkin, whom he knew.

'I thought you left your fire-watching job here in May,' the policeman said. 'I understood you to say you had another job nearer home, in Dalston. So what are you doing here?' It was now August. 'How did you get in anyway?'

'How did I get in? I used to work here, remember? I know my way in and out. I came to see if I'd left my old raincoat here by any chance. It's been lost or mislaid for three months now.'

After giving Dobkin a warning about the lights and showing him off the premises, the constable reported in to his superiors. This made very interesting reading for Detective Inspectors Hatton and Keeling. On 26 August they decided to ask Dobkin to assist them in their inquiries into the disappearance of Rachel Dobkin. Hatton took

Dobkin into the cellar where his wife's body had been found.

'PC Wakeley informs me that he saw you here on 4 August,' Hatton said.

'Who is PC Wakeley?'

'He is the regular beat policeman for the area. He says he has known you for some time, from when you used to be the firewatcher here.'

'Never heard of him,' replied Dobkin. 'I don't hobnob with coppers. And if a copper says he saw me here since I left the job, then he's a liar.'

Hatton took Dobkin back to the police station, where PC Wakeley was called from his desk. 'That's Harry Dobkin,' he said. 'I've often spoken to him about lights showing at the chapel. And I saw him there *after* he'd given up his job as firewatcher there.'

'That's a lie!' cried Dobkin. 'I've never seen him before in my life, and I wasn't there at any time after giving up my job!'

Harry Dobkin was then formally charged with the murder of his wife.

Dobkin's trial opened at the Old Bailey on 17 November 1942. He was defended by Mr F.H. Lawton, later to become Mr Justice Lawton. Mr L.A. Byrne prosecuted.

The main points of the trial hinged on the evidence of Professor Keith Simpson, the forensic pathologist, and on some discrepancies in the alleged height of the victim. It was the evidence of the broken bone in the throat which was brought into controversy. The prosecution counsel, who was young and comparatively inexperienced as a barrister at that time, sought to get the pathologist to admit that when a bomb fell and the blast exploded hurling broken masonry about, a person could be thrown violently forward and catch his or her voice-box on the edge of some sharp object and that this could cause a fracture of the right horn of the thyroid cartilage.

'I have seen injuries caused by such circumstances on many occasions,' the scientist replied, 'but the injuries were never confined to a fracture of the horn, which was the only injury in this case.' He went on to say that in fifteen years he had seen only one case where one horn *and one wing* were broken together, but never only the horn. During that time, he continued, he had examined over 11,000 cadavers, and the only time he had ever seen that particular injury was in cases of manual strangulation.

'And how many cases of manual strangulation have you examined?' Mr Byrne went on relentlessly. 'Fifty? Seventy?'

'It would run into several hundreds,' Professor Simpson replied. It was an answer calculated to stop the young prosecutor in his tracks and, had he wished to pursue the matter further, it could easily have been proved from the pathologist's meticulous case notes filed over fifteen years.

After Harry Dobkin had spent more than an entire day in the witness-box giving evidence in his own behalf, mostly to his own detriment, Miss Polly Dubinski, Rachel Dobkin's sister, was recalled by Mr Lawton. 'About twenty minutes ago,' he explained, 'a document of very great significance came into my possession, and I wish to question the witness on the matter.' Mr Lawton then produced a copy of the *News of the World* dated 4 May 1941, which ran a feature headed 'Missing from Home'. In this column there appeared a photograph of Rachel Dobkin, accompanied by her description. The photograph, with a description, had been supplied to the newspaper by Polly. In the published description Rachel's height had been given as 5ft. 3ins.

After Mr Lawton had the Home Office pathologist agreeing that, if the victim's height were indeed 5ft 3ins., then she could not be Rachel Dobkin, Polly Dubinski was then called to the stand. The very first thing she did was to deny that she had told the newspaper that her sister was 5ft. 3ins. in height. 'They must have made a mistake,' she insisted. 'I told them definitely that Rachel was about my own height – and I am 5ft. 1in. She was a little shorter than myself, if anything – certainly no taller. The newspaper got it wrong. After all, I am her sister, so I should know.' This was not what Mr Lawton had expected to hear, but it was enough to convince the jury. An application was then made to have Miss Dubinski measured, and a police-woman was detailed to do so. Polly was 4ft. 11½ins. in her stockinged feet, 5ft. 1in. tall with shoes. The case for the defence had collapsed over a matter of an inch and a half.

The jury was out for only twenty minutes before finding Harry Dobkin guilty of murdering his wife, and he was executed at Wandsworth Prison on 27 January 1943.

13

The Ice-cream Man Cometh

Tom Johnston, a detective with Los Angeles County Sheriff's Office in California, had no possible way of knowing, as he set out along the traffic-clogged Pasadena Freeway on 28 August 1982, that before the day was out he would be involved in the manhunt for a frenzied child sex killer. On arrival at his office in Pomona, he was greeted by his superior, Lieutenant Kurt Longfellow, with the news that prior to Tom Johnston's arrival at 8 p.m. a woman had called in on the 911 emergency line, her voice frantic, to report that her ten-year-old daughter, Robyn Leigh, had been missing for several hours. Longfellow quickly detailed Johnston to drive to the child's parents' home. 'Dear God,' he thought to himself as he accelerated hard, 'what a way to start the night shift!'

Johnston, on arriving at the modest house in a residential area of Baldwin Park, a predominantly working-class district, was told by Robyn's parents that she was a well-adjusted and happy little soul who was mature for her age, doing very well at school and had a wide circle of friends. She was very outgoing and friendly – a little too friendly, perhaps, but she had been given the usual warning about strangers.

Robyn's mother told Johnston that after supper she had asked for permission to go to her school, the Ernest R. Geddes Foundation Elementary School only a few yards from her home, to watch a baseball game. Tearfully, Mrs Leigh continued: 'I told her she could go, and my son went about half-way with her as he was going to meet a school friend. We both told her to be home before dark or she'd be in trouble.'

Johnston next interviewed a number of the family's neighbours. 'Robyn is a very sweet little girl, very friendly,' one said. 'She takes care of her little brothers and even helps her mother cook. She is a good student at school, too – never gets into any trouble.' Another neighbour said: 'Robyn's a friendly, affectionate girl who gets along with everybody. She's certainly not shy.'

Detective Johnston concluded in his own mind that the child had been abducted either along the way to the school playing-field, or at the playing-field itself. But of course he did not tell the distraught parents of his private fears. Instead, he assured them that the police would be immediately mounting an all-out search for the missing youngster. A team of detectives were at work within the hour, fanning out from the area and searching every possible place where a child, dead or alive, could be hidden, and asking innumerable questions of everyone they met along the way. No stone was left unturned: gardens, sheds, garages and other outbuildings were examined, and no one escaped the relentless questioning. Dogs were brought in and volunteer searchers rounded up. But midnight came and went, and the hunters had drawn a blank. Not a single clue had surfaced pointing to the whereabouts of the missing child.

At first light the following morning the search party of police officers and volunteers assembled outside the Leigh home in Phelan Avenue, Baldwin Park. The group included Robyn's schoolteachers and parents of her classmates, and when a number of Hell's Angels roared up on their powerful Harley-Davidson motorbikes and asked if they could join the volunteers, they were welcomed. Altogether the search party numbered about 100 strong.

Lieutenant Longfellow, who was in charge of the investigation, detailed the party to comb an area of woods and brush clumps which covered about four square miles around the Baldwin Park district. No clues were found, and plans were immediately made to make an aerial search by police helicopter, taking in not only Baldwin Park but also Pasadena, El Monte, San Gabriel and Arcadia. Meanwhile a recent photograph of Robyn was given to Lieutenant Longfellow, who had copies made for all the sheriff's officers and patrolmen all the way along the coast of California from Los Angeles to Capistrano Beach. Copies were also given to the news media.

At about 3 a.m. in the morning of the following day, while the posses of detectives and volunteers were still searching in desolate outlying areas of scrub and wasteland, a call came through to HQ from a man who had been out walking his dogs when, he reported, he had seen a man in an ice-cream van stop the vehicle and throw a 'pale object' into one of the concrete flood-control channels of the Eaton Wash, off Orange Grove Boulevard in Pasadena, after which he made off at speed. The caller decided to investigate, and to his horror he found the naked body of a little girl.

A dispatcher at HQ looked at his chart to ascertain the whereabouts of the nearest patrol car in that area, and detailed the patrolman to check the report. Two minutes later the car skidded to a stop by the side of a fenced-off drainage ditch. The location was ten miles from Robyn Leigh's home.

The owner of the dogs was told to wait at the scene and not to allow anyone except police to approach the area while the patrolman radioed for back-up. Shortly afterwards detectives, accompanied by deputies and technicians, arrived, followed a few minutes later by Detective Tom Johnston and the coroner. Johnston said that Lieutenant Longfellow would be arriving as soon as possible, and in fact he arrived within ten minutes. Johnston briefed him on what he had been told by the man who had found the body.

'There was no doubt in my mind as to who the girl was,' the man said. 'Her picture and description were on the late television news. I knew it was her.'

'Thank God for men who walk their dogs at 2 a.m.,' Longfellow commented. 'She could have drifted off, gotten snagged in a culvert, anything. Then it could have been months before she was found.'

The body was a sight to sicken hardened police officers. Her face was contorted into a look of abject terror and pain, while her slender body was a mass of bruises and abrasions, mainly in the area of the buttocks and that part of the chest where the breasts had not yet begun to form. The coroner said that there were no marks of a ligature on her neck. He added that it was highly probable that Robyn had been sexually assaulted, but that this would have to be confirmed by the autopsy. The body, after being photographed *in situ*, was taken to the morgue, and the autopsy arranged for the following afternoon.

The coroner's theory was confirmed by the autopsy findings. The child had been savagely raped both vaginally and anally, causing severe trauma to the perineum and massive injuries to the rectum and the vagina. The cause of death was suffocation, most probably by a hand clamped over the child's mouth and nose, followed by a violent blow to the head. It was theorized that the child was still alive when she was thrown into the storm channel and had, apparently, struck her head against the concrete slope.

Meanwhile detectives continued to examine the immediate area where the body was found for clues, but did not come up with a single lead. The case was proving most frustrating. The man who had found the body had been too far away at the time of sighting the man in the ice-cream van to be able to give the police a description of the driver, or even much more than a very sketchy description of the van. There were hundreds of similar vans operating in California in the long, hot summer.

Door-to-door inquiries were resumed, and pedestrians and motorists alike stopped and questioned. Lieutenant Longfellow also detailed his men to go over the crime scene again, with a fine-tooth comb. 'The crime scene is the last place the killer had contact with the victim,' he said, 'and the closest we will come to him until we actually catch him. Pick up every cigarette end, piece of paper, matchstick – the most unimportant-looking object might be the evidence that breaks the case.'

The breakthrough which was to solve the identity of the killer came in quite a different and unexpected way. Based on the statement of the man who had been walking his dogs that it was definitely an ice-cream van that he had seen, detectives decided to contact every ice-cream vending company in the area and run a check on all their operators. During the course of this investigation, they made a startling discovery – a convicted child sex offender was employed as an ice-cream vendor in the area, unbeknown to his parole officer. This job, like any other involving contact with children, is forbidden to paroled offenders in this category. And the route of his regular run included Phelan Avenue, where both Robyn Leigh's home and the school she attended, the Ernest R. Geddes Foundation Elementary School, were situated.

A perusal of the police computer records showed that the man, forty-two-year-old Robert Stansbury, had a history of convictions, mostly for sex offences against minors, and had served six years in San Quentin for raping an eight-year-old girl. He had been released on parole in September 1981.

The owner of the van driven by Stansbury, who was a partner in the vending company, was located. He told detectives that he knew that Stansbury was an ex-convict but that he did not know what offence he had served time for. He also did not know that Stansbury had taken the job without the knowledge of his parole officer.

On 30 September 1982, armed with arrest and search warrants issued by a municipal court judge, a contingent of police officers visited Stansbury's home in Pomona. They took him into custody without resistance, and he was booked into the Los Angeles County jail, where he was charged with the murder of Robyn Leigh. He denied all knowledge of the child's death.

Further investigation revealed that Stansbury, who was well-known to many of the children at the school, had frequently offered free ice-cream and lollipops to several of the younger girls – never to the boys. Two witnesses told the investigators that Robyn had told them that 'the ice-cream man had given her free ice-cream three or four times.' From this it was apparent that Stansbury had deliberately sought to win Robyn's confidence in order to make it easier for him to carry out his plan to abduct her at some time when other children were not there to see him do so.

Police at Stansbury's apartment found a number of cardboard boxes hidden in a closet. One of them contained at least fifty pairs of little girls' panties and briefs, all obviously used. Another of the boxes contained photographs of little girls, some just ordinary snapshots, others in varying stages of undress, and a few nude. A

Polaroid camera and films were also found.

The forensic pathologist who had carried out the autopsy on Robyn's body stated at the preliminary hearing that the body had been subjected to intense cold prior to being dumped in the storm channel, as though she had been kept in a deep-freeze such as the kind found in an ice-cream vendor's van. Police theorized that the body had been hastily stowed into the deep-freeze after the rape, until the accused felt that it was safe to drive out to the Eaton Wash area to dispose of it.

After lengthy mental evaluations, Robert Stansbury was found competent to stand trial. The selection and empanellment of a jury was completed early in March 1985. Six men and six women were eventually chosen. Stansbury sat quietly in court during the trial, looking as unconcerned as a man waiting for a bus. He pleaded not guilty, and elected to defend himself in court, spurning the offer of a court-appointed attorney.

Stansbury did not deny that he knew Robyn Leigh, and when it was put to him that he had given her free ice-cream on several occasions in order to win her confidence, he replied that he was 'fond of children' and that he did not recall having treated Robyn Leigh any differently from the other children in the playground. The evidence put forward by several child witnesses, however, soon demolished this line of defence, and Deputy District Attorney Richard Burns, the prosecutor, showed how Stansbury had singled out the pretty ten-year-old as his potential victim from the very first, and had travelled to the school playground every afternoon for several weeks to offer her free ice-cream as a bait to win her confidence.

Stansbury showed no emotion as the Superior Court jury's verdict was read, finding him guilty of kidnap, rape and murder, assault and battery and aggravated sodomy, and on 15 July 1985, after a three-month trial, he was sentenced to die in the gas chamber in San Quentin.

As the prisoner was led from the court between two armed guards he still looked as self-assured and arrogant as he had done throughout the entire trial. For the mother of the victim, weeping uncontrollably, he did not so much as spare a glance, or even say 'I'm sorry.' All he said, to a court official as they led him down, was, 'There will be a new trial, that's for sure. No two ways about it.' But there has been no new trial, and Robert Stansbury is still on death row in San Quentin Prison.

14

The Bogus G-Man

When an elderly widow named Erna Hoediker was found dead on 3 January 1984 in her modest apartment in the Tempelhof district of West Berlin, police attributed the killing – for murder it was without a shadow of doubt – to some teenaged burglar who had somehow tricked his way into her home, possibly on the pretext of doing some odd jobs for her, and then killing her so that she would not be able to identify him. Unfortunately, as the police well knew, this kind of thing was on the increase.

Frau Hoediker's body was discovered by her friend of long standing, Frau Ilse Warnecke, who lived a few doors away. The two women were in the habit of visiting one another almost every day; Frau Warnecke was only three years younger than her friend, who was eighty-seven years of age. They had known each other for more than fifty years.

Although Frau Warnecke had a key to her friend's apartment she had not needed to use it, for she found the door ajar. This was most unusual – Frau Hoediker would never normally leave her door unlocked. Knowing, therefore, that something must be wrong, she entered with a certain degree of trepidation. She was, however, scarcely prepared for the shock of discovering, not only that the apartment had been ransacked, but her friend lying face down in the bath, which was three-quarters full of cold water. What kind of a fiend could have done this? She wasted no time wondering, but closed the door and made for the café at the end of the block where she could telephone the police.

Uniformed officers from the Tempelhof precinct responded immediately to the call and were soon at the apartment. They observed that the entire place had been frenziedly turned over in a search for money and valuables. The dead woman's friend told the officers that Frau Hoediker had not been very well-off and that she thought her savings amounted to the equivalent of some £150, which she kept in her home as 'she did not trust banks'. She also had a few modest pieces of jewellery. A thorough search by detectives failed to turn up any cash at all, nor did they find the semi-precious gems.

The police were certain that robbery was the motive, since the body of the dead woman was fully clothed and there had been no sexual interference of any kind. The body was taken to the police morgue and the pathologist who carried out the autopsy established that Frau Hoediker had been already dead – by manual strangulation – before she had been put into the bath, so drowning was not the cause of death. The time of the murder was calculated at about 7 p.m. the previous evening.

Some unidentified fingerprints were found in the apartment, in addition to those of the late occupier and of her friend. The presence of unidentified prints seemed to imply that the killer was not a known criminal, otherwise his prints would have been on file, and this lent credence to the 'teenage burglar' theory. Frau Warnecke made a statement, in which she averred that her friend had lived in Berlin all her life and that she would never, in any circumstances, have opened her door to a stranger, much less allowed him over the threshold, so the murderer must have broken in. Frau Warnecke was undoubtedly telling the truth about her friend's caution, but the police knew that no one had broken into the apartment. There were no fewer than three locks on the front door, including a chain lock, and all the windows had been locked on the inside. None of the locks or windows had been tampered with. The killer must have been allowed into the apartment by Frau Hoediker, and when he had left he had left the door unlocked.

The police noted the manner in which the apartment had been ransacked, with furniture and fittings overturned, drawers removed bodily from chests, the contents thrown haphazardly on the floor, boxes, jars, bottles, even kitchen storage bins upended – all signs of a frenzied rummaging. Nothing had been taken but money and the few semi-precious jewellery items, according to Frau Warnecke's statement. This, in police opinion, pointed to the thief being a drug addict desperate for money to obtain a 'fix' – and there was no dearth of drug addicts, especially teenaged ones, in that part of Berlin. Such desperate persons would be likely to employ desperate measures such as robbing defenceless old ladies who would offer little physical resistance owing to age or infirmity, rather than setting up a common-or-garden robbery such as a shop hold-up to grab money from the till. (Shopkeepers in high-crime areas would be likely to keep a handgun under the counter or, if not, at the very least a cosh or club.)

The police ran in a number of known drug addicts off the street, but no one seemed to know anything which could provide even a slight lead. Warnings were issued on television, radio and in newspapers to elderly persons living alone not to allow anyone into their homes without proof of identification.

All these warnings must have gone unheeded for, only eleven days after Erna Hoediker had been strangled and left in her bath, another widow, eighty-one-year-old Hilde Baumgartner, was found strangled in her apartment by her friend, seventy-four-year-old Krystina Buehl, who had gone to visit her at 142 Birkenstrasse, in the Tiergarten district. Police called to the scene arrived in less than fifteen minutes. Frau Buehl informed them that her friend kept the equivalent of about £800 at home 'as she was not very keen on banks'. Detectives tut-tutted among themselves once more: why were old folks so paranoid about keeping their money safely in a bank? Was it just that they liked to have the reassuring feel of the folded notes, rather than an impersonal-looking cheque-book and a plastic card?

The detectives working on the two cases noticed the similarities immediately: both women had been manually strangled; their homes had been burgled with ferocious intensity and only money and jewellery had been taken; and no forcible entry to the premises had been used. The inevitable conclusion was that the killer's only motive was money and that the murders were purely to stop the

victims from identifying him as no sexual element was
involved.

When on 31 January – seventeen days after the murder
of Hilde Baumgartner – seventy-nine-year-old Jutta
Kreutzer was found strangled in her apartment at 74
Detmolderstrasse, in the Wilmersdorf district, the police
were able to add another point to the *modus operandi* of the
unknown killer. Each of the killings had taken place in a
different police district. On the face of it, it seemed
possible that the murderer was deliberately choosing a
different district for his operations on each occasion.

Frau Kreutzer had been found because the killer had left
the door to her apartment ajar and, in a city like Berlin,
this was a thing one just doesn't do. Leaving one's front
door open was an invitation to any passing petty thief,
never mind a homicidal burglar. Even if an occupier were
merely visiting the tenant of an adjoining flat, he or she
would lock the door and take the key. So when a tenant on
the same floor, who did not even know Frau Kreutzer
except by sight, saw the open door, she knew immediately
that something was wrong. This lady was an avid
newspaper-reader and was fully aware of the two murders
of old women in the city. She did not enter the open
apartment but rushed back to her own flat and, in
understandable panic, shot all the bolts and mortice
deadlocks before calling the police. From her reading of
the reports she knew that the killer did not strike twice in
the same area – at least up to date – but, she reasoned, it
was best to be on the safe side …

It was subsequently found that the dead woman's
assets in the form of cash kept in the house amounted to
little more than the equivalent of £350, and she had no
jewellery except a diamond ring and a gold wedding
band, both of which had been wrenched from her finger.
The apartment was in the most appalling disorder, literally
torn apart in the killer's frantic search. Again there was no
indication of forcible entry.

The police now co-ordinated a team drawn from each of
the districts involved. It was realized, almost from the
start, that these killings formed a series and were the work
of one man. What was puzzling them was the apparent
ease with which he had been able to enter their homes,

seemingly without question. It was almost impossible that any elderly women in the city had failed to become aware of the warnings in the media. The warnings had certainly failed to scare off the killer, for on 5 February – less than a week after the murder of Jutta Kreutzer – seventy-seven-year-old Maria Dietsche was found strangled in her tiny flatlet at 44 Naumannstrasse, in the Schönberg precinct. It had been a high price to pay for her meagre savings of the equivalent of £50 in German marks which a friend was able to inform police was all she kept in her home and probably all she had. Wherever she had hidden it, it was gone when detectives examined her ransacked abode. She had no jewellery.

Elderly women living alone in Berlin were now in a state of panic and literally barricaded themselves in their homes, refusing to open the door unless they recognized the caller's voice. Just to open the door might be taking one's life in one's hands. The police were stymied. The killer left no identifiable clues, his fingerprints were not on file, and he never struck twice in the same district. The only definite thing the police knew about him was that he was in desperate need of money – so desperate that he did not stop at murder to conceal his tracks. And the pathologist who had conducted the autopsies on all four victims had determined that the stranglings had been carried out by an adult male: the killer was no teenage boy with small or weak hands. Inquiries at jewellers' and pawn shops had not located any of the missing items; the thief was obviously biding his time. This tended to lessen the drug addict theory to a certain extent, although it was not ruled out.

Police decided to interrogate uniformed men such as postmen, gas and electricity meter readers and so on. Old ladies might well open the door if such a person could show her his identification and wore a uniform. The majority of the apartment doors were fitted with chain bolts which allowed an opening of a couple of inches or so but did not unlock the door. Others were fitted with 'spyglass' peep-holes. This theory was rendered more plausible when it was realized that three of the murdered women's apartment doors had chain-locks and the fourth was fitted with a spy-hole.

As against this hypothesis, a man in uniform is more conspicuous than one in ordinary clothes. So detectives made inquiries of apartment building superintendents, janitors, cleaners, boilermen, caretakers and so on, in the hope that someone might have seen such a uniformed man visiting flats in their block. None reported having seen such a person at any relevant time.

On 12 February – one week after Maria Dietsche had been found dead – a twenty-four-year-old woman went to visit her grandmother Käthe Heidemann, who resided at 61 Thomasstrasse, in the Neuköln district. She was eighty-three years old and fairly comfortably off, but unfortunately, despite her better education and circumstances, she still shared with her less well-off contemporaries the notion that banks were to be avoided, and was known to have kept her entire life savings, which would have amounted to more than £7000 in English money, in cash at home. Several relatives, including her granddaughter, had advised her that this was a very foolish thing to do, but the old lady stubbornly resisted all this well-meaning advice and continued to keep her nest-egg in several different hiding-places in her apartment. This devious ploy, however, did not deter the unknown killer from finding every last pfennig, after he had first strangled his victim and turned her apartment inside out from top to bottom. A jewellery casket was also emptied and the contents removed, but no one who knew Frau Heidemann was aware of the exact value of the gems. The door had been left open, as in the previous cases; it was as though the killer wanted the crime to be discovered easily.

Now, for the first time, a clue surfaced. In the course of their door-to-door inquiries in the adjoining blocks, a woman in her early eighties told a detective that someone had rung her door bell on the evening of 10 February. She opened the door and saw standing outside in the hall a neatly-dressed, good-looking man in his early twenties. Tall and well-built, he had shown her a badge bearing the words 'New York, N.Y.' and 'FBI Special Agent'. She wondered what an American FBI agent could be doing in Berlin, and asked him, to which he replied that he was looking for a gang of international terrorists and that they were suspected of hiding in a building which was overlooked by one of the windows in her apartment. He had called to request her permission to enter the apartment to scan the building in question with the binoculars which he had hanging round his neck, but hidden under his clothing.

The woman had accepted the man's story as genuine, and was about to slide the chain-lock off the door, when her nephew, who was staying with her, appeared from behind her, entering the hall from the kitchen. He was a tall man in his thirties. He asked the old lady what the man wanted; the latter then said that he had forgotten his official notebook – he'd left it in the car – and he'd be right back. He then left hurriedly, and had never returned.

The inspector in charge of the investigation felt something click into place as he read this latest report. He now knew exactly how this man gained his victims' confidence, playing on their vulnerability, their gullibility and their trust, as he preyed on them systematically and without mercy for his own ends. His victims were familiar with the G-men in the old American movies they had been watching on television for years; they knew, too, of international terrorism and the lengths to which governments will go to search these men out. Consequently they had naïvely trusted the man from the FBI. What they did not know, of course, was that these replica badges could be purchased by mail-order by anybody – advertised in many popular American magazines which were on sale everywhere in Berlin. These copies were close approximations to the real thing, with minor differences just sufficient to render their sale legal to 'collectors', as their advertisers put it.

Another question which concerned the investigators was: how did this man choose his victims? Did he follow elderly women home from shopping trips? Did he just ring door bells at random? In the latter case, there must have been several calls where he discovered that the woman was not living alone. Several people must have had a good look at him, and they had a good description from the woman and her nephew from the neighbourhood of the last victim. The detectives decided to step up their door-to-door inquiries. They realized that this man was as wily as the most dedicated professional criminal, with all the professional criminal's cunning. He had deliberately avoided striking twice in the same area precisely because he was fully convinced that the police would not make inquiries outside those areas. So that was what the detectives now decided to do. He had not believed that they would bother to question tenants in other blocks where no murders had taken place, and he was not taking any chances on persons in the buildings where he had committed his crimes seeing him and describing him and his bogus FBI badge. But he had underestimated the police ...

The massive investigation paid off. They came up with a number of cases where the caller had been confronted with two or more persons living in an apartment and he had made some excuse and left. In one or two isolated cases, however, old ladies living alone had been too scared, even of a purported FBI agent, to let him in. One of them had called the caretaker, who had rapidly appeared on the scene and told the man to leave the premises in no uncertain terms. This proved the breakthrough for the investigators.

The caretaker reported that, after seeing the young man off the premises, he had watched him walk down the street and enter a tavern. Shown a composite identikit-style picture of the suspect, the innkeeper said that he knew the man well as he was a regular, and that his first name was Waldemar, although he did not know his last name or his address. He also confirmed that he had come in for a couple of beers on the evening in question. The innkeeper thought that the man might live in the Mariensdorf district, having overheard him animatedly discussing with another customer housing availability and rent levels in that area. Police attempts to identify and trace this customer led nowhere. It was significant, however, that no calls had been made by the self-styled G-man anywhere in that area.

The police were now a little nearer, but they were not near enough. On 23 February the caretaker of an apartment block in the Charlottenburg district saw that the door to one of the flats stood ajar as he went on his morning security rounds. Entering, he found the tenant, Käthe Dreichler, strangled amid the shambles of her once neat home. Käthe was seventy-four. Her savings, the equivalent of £400, were gone, along with the rings and the wristwatch she had been wearing. The bogus G-man had been careless enough to leave a complete set of clear fingerprints on the inside door handle. These matched some of the unidentified prints found in other flats. This fellow obviously disliked wearing gloves …

The police had now traced the customer to whom the suspect had been seen talking by the innkeeper. It had certainly taken them some time, but the customer had been completely unaware that he could have been of considerable assistance to the police and, had he only known that he could have helped bring the killer of the old ladies to justice, he would have come forward voluntarily. He said that the man he had been talking to was Waldemar Szczepiński, a Pole who had become a naturalized German, who lived in Mariensdorf. The tavern customer was able to give the police his exact address, where detectives found him and took him into custody unresisting. At the time of his arrest he was wearing the bogus FBI badge, and the binoculars were found in his apartment along with an official-looking notebook and self-propelling pencil attached to it with a leather thong.

Under intensive interrogation, Szczepiński quickly confessed to the murders. His fingerprints matched the set found at the scene of his last crime and also some of the ones found at previous crime locations. Asked why he had been robbing old ladies, the theory of the drug addict was quickly proved wrong. He told police that in the preceding September he had lost his job and had no means of keeping up the payments on the apartment he and his wife were purchasing in the up-market Mariensdorf suburb.They had a two-year-old child, and another was on the way. His wife had no inkling that he had lost his job as a security guard – he continued to come and go at the hours he normally kept when in employment. He did not want to worry her, he explained.

A life sentence – which is what he received – in West Germany rarely means much more than about ten years in prison, and as Waldemar Szczepiński will still be only thirty-two in 1994 (ten years on), it may well be the old ladies of Berlin who will be worried rather than his wife.

15
'I Got Another One Today'

Donald Harvey was a hospital attendant and nurses' aide at the Daniel Drake Memorial Hospital, a publicly-owned medical faculty in Cincinnati, Ohio. His duties were carried out in a ward for elderly and terminally ill patients. He had joined the staff of the hospital in 1985 straight from his previous position at the Veterans' Administration Medical Center, also in Cincinnati, where he had been a morgue attendant for the previous ten years. Towards the end of his employment there officials had suspected him of stealing body tissue from the morgue, but rather than pursue criminal charges against him they had quietly allowed him to resign. They wished to have no scandal attached to their establishment with its inevitable consequence of distress for the bereaved families.

Harvey had managed to conceal the facts surrounding his severance from the Veterans' Administration Medical Center, and had even succeeded in obtaining from them a reference, which merely stated that he had been employed by the Center for ten years.

Harvey settled into his new position with alacrity. A few of the nurses noticed that their new colleague seemed to have a morbid fascination with death, but then that was, perhaps, to be expected of a man who had worked in a mortuary for ten years. Now, in a ward for the elderly and terminally ill, death occurred fairly frequently as a matter of course. Some of the patients were in their eighties or nineties while others, younger in some cases, had cancer or other irreversible conditions. A fatal stroke or a heart attack, was, if not an everyday occurrence, so common-place in a ward of this nature as to be accepted as a matter of course. 'They come and they go,' Harvey was heard to observe on one such occasion.

1985 saw some come and some go, but for some reason, not apparent to the nurses, more came and went during 1986, and the turnover increased alarmingly in 1987. No one could remember so many patients dying at such frequent intervals. The nurses started to be more alert and watch for anything unusual which might be a contributing factor to the unusually high number of deaths in their ward. They watched the nurses' aides and attendants, including Harvey, but except for finding that all the deaths occurred when Harvey was on duty, they could not pin-point any particular cause. Harvey, they noted, appeared to care for his patients with great concern and was the epitome of kindness, but he still had more fatalities on his duty rounds than anyone else. The nurses began to rag him and nicknamed him 'the kiss of death', to which he responded with a laugh and joined in the humorous banter. 'I got another one today,' he said whenever a patient died. The nurses took it as the macabre joke of an ex-mortician.

By the time 1987 was well under way, however, a number of the nurses got together to talk about Donald Harvey. The jokes were now wearing rather thin, and one of the nurses said that she thought there was more in them than met the eye. A small deputation of them decided to go to their superiors, who dismissed their suspicions as 'a lot of hogwash' and told them that frequent death of patients were to be expected in a ward for the aged and terminally ill. As for Harvey, he had worked in a mortuary for ten years before coming to the hospital, and like many morticians he had what was called a 'gallows sense of humour'.

Things would probably have continued as they were indefinitely had not another patient died, towards the end of March. This was not an elderly or terminally sick person but a forty-four-year-old motorcyclist named John Powell, who had received severe injuries in a motorcycle crash. He had remained in a coma for several days without regaining consciousness before his death. It was decided to perform an autopsy on his body.

At this autopsy, the county pathologist noticed an odour like that of bitter almonds emanating from the body as soon as he opened it. The specialist knew that this

odour denoted cyanide of potassium, and upon making the
requisite tests he soon came up with positive proof that
cyanide had been administered to Powell and that it was
this and not the injuries sustained in the crash that had
caused his death. Someone had poisoned the patient as he
lay in hospital. But who?

It was not, of course, the task of the pathologist to make
inquiries but that of the police, who were soon busy
interviewing all the staff. Every person who had been in
contact with John Powell was questioned, and it was
ascertained that Donald Harvey had been the last person to
have been seen tending the man before he died. He had
also been heard to tell a nurse, 'He won't last more than a
day or two,' despite the fact that a doctor who had
examined him had said that Powell had a good chance of
recovery although it might take a considerable time.

During the course of police investigations, a number of
nurses voiced their private suspicions regarding Donald
Harvey in connection with the unusual frequency of deaths
in their ward. It was decided to invite all members of staff to
submit to a polygraph (lie-detector) test. All agreed to
participate except Donald Harvey, who refused. 'Why
bother with a lie-detector test?' he replied. 'I can tell you
who killed that motorcyclist with cyanide. It was me.'

Taken into custody, Harvey confessed to twenty-one
murders in the hospital. He used a number of different
methods of killing, which is unusual for a serial killer; such
multiple murderers mostly stick to one method, such as
strangling, poisoning, shooting and so on. But Donald
Harvey cheerfully confessed to administering lethal doses
of such poisons as cyanide of potassium, prussic acid,
arsenic and rat poison, and powerful drugs such as digitalis
which are lethal in large amounts. Then, on occasions, he
would vary the pattern by administering hepatitis germs,
injecting air into the veins to cause fatal embolisms, or even
suffocating the victim with a plastic bag over the head.

In addition, Harvey confessed to killing his landlady,
Mrs Helen Metzger, on 10 April 1983 by giving her a pie
laced with arsenic, and killing the father of his room-mate
by giving him the same poison in a pudding. He had also
given this to his room-mate's mother at the same time, but
she survived.

On Tuesday, 18 August 1987, Donald Harvey, thirty-five, stood trial in Hamilton County Court, before Judge William S. Matthews. The county prosecutor, Arthur Ney, had as his opponent William P. Whalen, Harvey's attorney. After reading out the long list of Harvey's victims, he derided the accused man's explanation that he had snuffed out the lives of twenty-one hospital patients in his care as 'mercy killings'. 'The accused is no mercy killer,' he boomed. 'He's not insane, either. He killed because he liked to kill. He enjoyed it!'

Grim-faced relatives of the dead packed the courtroom. Not all were very pleased at learning that the prosecution had accepted a plea-bargain, with the result that in return for a full confession Harvey would be spared Ohio's death penalty. 'Without the confession,' Ney explained, 'the case could have crumbled for lack of concrete evidence.' He pointed out that the victims, all of whom had been buried, had first been embalmed, and that because of this the bodies would have been unlikely to show traces of poisons or other noxious substances administered to them. Also, he added, no one at the hospital had ever seen Harvey act in an improper manner. Little question had ever been raised about the deaths, because all the victims except John Powell had either been elderly or terminally ill.

Ney then went on to point out that Powell fitted neither of those categories but was killed nevertheless, and that Harvey's former landlady and the parents of his room-mate had all been middle-aged and in good health, which effectively scotched the notion that Harvey was a 'mercy killer'.

The greatest shock to the kin of the victims who attended Harvey's trial was in hearing the evidence of some of their number, who described the accused as having been kind and sympathetic both towards the patients in his care and to their visiting relatives. 'He was always smiling and considerate,' one said. Another, a sixty-nine-year-old widow, described how when her late husband had been admitted to the hospital after a stroke which had left him blind, Harvey had done everything she could have asked for regarding the physical and emotional comfort of the patient. 'He was so nice, always helping in every way possible,' she said.

One woman stated that he should die in the gas chamber. 'He meted out death,' she said, 'so death should be meted out to him.' Another woman said, 'Nobody has the right to decide who will live and who will die. Only God has that right.' And the daughter of a man whom Harvey suffocated to death said vehemently: 'They say he'll rot in prison. That's too good for him.'

Three consecutive life imprisonment terms of thirty years meant that he would not have a snowflake's chance in hell of parole before he was ninety-five. That is, if he – unlike some of his late victims – lived that long. But one thing would be certain: if he did, and was released from prison at the age of ninety-five, at least he would never get a job in a hospital again.

16
Heavy Metal

It is said that the line of distinction between genius and madness is a very thin one, and this was certainly true of Graham Young. If the processes of his mind had developed in the normal manner from his early boyhood, instead of becoming warped and distorted somewhere along the line, he would certainly have become a genius in chemistry, mathematics and physics. His headmaster said so and his other teachers testified to this conclusion. Instead, the youthful 'whizz kid' of the chemistry laboratory found his fascination with his subject distorted into a deadly obsession which led him, first to Broadmoor, the secure hospital for the criminally insane, and finally to prison.

At the age of nine, the interest which was eventually to dominate Graham Young's entire life was already clearly in evidence. He rarely played with other children of his own age, but preferred talking to adults on serious subjects. He would seek out pensioners sitting on the benches in the park to talk to, rather than playing with other boys on the nearby swings and roundabouts. Often the old men and women did not have the faintest idea what this precocious boy was talking about, what with the long words and scientific terms, and the subjects which went right over their heads.

One day his stepmother and his aunt noticed that bottles of perfume and nail varnish were disappearing from their dressing-tables. They didn't solve the mystery of the missing bottles until one day his stepmother spotted a hole in his jacket pocket and set to with needle and cotton to mend it. To her astonishment, she found in the pocket not only one of the missing nail varnish bottles but also a half-empty bottle of acid and a phial of ether. She tackled him with these finds, and he made no excuses.

The ether, he said, he liked to sniff; as to the other two items, he needed them because he was conducting some chemical experiments. He said that he obtained the acid and the ether from the dustbins outside a chemist's shop in Neasden, London, where he lived. Mrs Young went to warn the chemist concerned, who said he would be more careful as to what he threw in the dustbin in future. 'What?' he said. 'The boy is only *nine*?'

For the first time, Graham's parents now found cause to worry about him. Molly Young, his stepmother, started to take more than a cursory interest in the library books he was borrowing, which he kept in his room and never brought downstairs. To her horror, she found them all to be about Hitler, the war, Nazism, black magic and horror-science fiction. Hardly the kind of reading a nine-year-old boy should be interested in. She decided to have a word with the librarian, who told her that it was quite normal for young boys to be interested in the war and militarism, though she admitted that black magic and the occult was not suitable reading for children. She said she would try to discourage Graham from borrowing such books, but said she could not stop junior members from borrowing adult books.

Graham's interest in Hitler and the policies of Nazi Germany continued unabated; after all, he pointed out, the war had only been over ten years (it was 1956) and 'at that time I was only a baby so I could not enjoy it.' *Enjoy* it? This child was certainly most peculiar, Molly mused. Fancy coming out with a remark like that! Then Graham found an old swastika badge which he insisted on wearing, much to his father's annoyance. He was becoming more and more obsessive. With his unhealthy interests, he had nothing whatever in common with his contemporaries.

Chemistry and medicine were now looming larger in his library book choice. Molly heard vague but unsubstantiated rumours that her stepson was carrying out various unspecified 'experiments' on mice and even cats, but she was never able to find anything to prove this and she did not like to ask him if he knew anything about the cats that had mysteriously disappeared from his neighbours' gardens. If he had been instrumental in getting rid of a few mice, they were not going to complain. But the boy was so secretive these days ...

Two years passed, and Graham Young passed his eleven-plus with flying colours. His teachers enthused over this student with his passion for chemistry, physics and maths – the first two of which he would only now begin studying in school. All his knowledge was self-taught. This was clearly no ordinary child. 'He will go far,' his headmaster said. In only three years' time, they would all know exactly how far he would go ...

Meanwhile, as a reward for passing his eleven-plus, his father gave him a chemistry set – an ironic choice, as subsequent events showed. Graham moved to his new secondary school in Willesden, where his science master, Geoffrey Hughes, found his work most impressive and placed him in the 'A' stream. He was given a free hand in the laboratory and, together with two school friends, Clive Creager and Christopher Williams, who shared his interest in chemistry, he would perform experiments on mice, injecting them with various concoctions and studying their reactions until they died. Graham would then perform a post-mortem, taking his friends through all the orthodox procedures while they marvelled at his knowledge. Once he took a dead mouse home to perform an autopsy in his room; Molly Young was horrified and made him throw it in the dustbin.

He appeared to be very upset by his stepmother's action, and rushed upstairs to his room and slammed the door. Drawing was one of his interests, and he spent the next hour or so at this pursuit. The next morning when he left for school he contrived to leave a drawing on the hallstand without anyone seeing him. The sketch was of a tombstone at the head of a grave in the cemetery. On the tombstone was the inscription 'In Hateful Memory of Molly Young. R.I.P.' On another occasion when he had been reproved for some misdemeanour, he left a drawing depicting two coffins, on which were the names of his father and stepmother. His school friend Clive Creager was later to recollect that frequently in class he surreptitiously made sketches instead of reading his school textbooks. These drawings, Creager said, often showed people hanging from a gallows, suspended over a vat of acid, or with syringes marked 'Poison' sticking in their bodies. Yet no one at the time heeded these warning signs of an unbalanced mind, attributing them merely to a childish over-reaction to the macabre horror comics he was so fond of reading.

By the age of twelve Graham Young knew more about toxicology – the science of poisons – than most laymen are conversant with in a lifetime; his knowledge of this subject even compared favourably with that possessed by the average GP who does not specialize in this area of medicine. Most of his library books were now about toxicology, forensic medicine and famous poisoners, Hitler and the Nazis having taken a back seat. His chemical expertise was astounding for a twelve-year-old boy: he could reel off the constituents of any popular patent medicine, and knew the medical names of common ailments. Frequently he offered advice to members of his family, neighbours and friends on how to treat minor illnesses. He had a phenomenal memory for detail with total recall.

But it was poison that most fascinated Graham Young. In a discussion with classmates in which boys were asked what careers they wanted to pursue after school, his friends said they thought of becoming engine drivers, salesmen, dentists and the like, but Graham said that his ambition was to become a famous poisoner, like Crippen or Dr Pritchard. 'One day,' he boasted openly to his schoolmates, 'my name will be as infamous as theirs.' Of course the boys laughed it off and said that Graham certainly had a weird sense of humour …

The echoes of his friends' laughter were still reverberating around the classroom when Graham (now thirteen) went into Geoffrey Reis's chemist's shop in Neasden High Street and asked for twenty-five grains of antimony, which he had discovered from his studies was a slow-acting poison which caused death only if administered regularly over a sustained period of time. Its presenting symptoms are vomiting, stomach pain and cramp – symptoms which are also characteristic of many common illnesses.

The minimum legal age for purchasing poisons on the restricted list was seventeen. Reis questioned this

young-looking boy, who informed him that he was
seventeen. Reis asked him what he wanted the antimony
for, and the 'young-looking boy' described a series of
chemical experiments he had in mind in minute technical
detail. 'He knew more about the chemical properties of
antimony than I did,' the chemist later admitted. 'I
thought him rather small for his age, but his knowledge
convinced me that he was much older than he looked. I
sold him the poison.'

Graham received half a crown pocket money weekly
from his father and he supplemented this with a cleaning
job at a local café, for which he received five shillings a
week. With this money he purchased various chemical
substances for his experiments, including poisons. He
went to various chemists' shops in the area, signing the
poisons register in the name of 'M.E. Evans' and giving a
false address. He was able to build up a stock of antimony,
a phial of which he carried around with him in a pocket,
and he even kept a small bottle of it in his desk at school.
He would take it out and show it to his friends. 'He would
often take it out of his desk and pass it round,' Clive
Creager recalled. 'He called it "his little friend". We all
thought he was up the creek. Crackers. Most of us didn't
believe it was poison anyway. We thought it was just
coloured water and he was having us on.'

Christopher Williams had been Young's closest chum at
school, and Young brooked no apparent transfer of
allegiance to another boy as his best friend. Williams
started going around with another student named
Terence Hands, which annoyed Graham so much that he
challenged Williams to a fight. Graham was no match for
Williams, who was taller and stronger, and soon found
himself lying flat on his back with the bigger boy standing
over him. His pride was hurt rather than his body. 'I'll kill
you for this!' he gritted through clenched teeth. The other
boy just laughed at the time, but he had cause to
remember it later. 'It was a fair fight,' was his only
comment at the time. 'I've beaten you fair and square.'

A week later, Williams suddenly started vomiting
uncontrollably in class, and was allowed to go home. The
next day he was perfectly well. But a week later the same
thing happened again. Williams remembered that on each

occasion the vomiting occurred during afternoon lessons, after he had shared a sandwich lunch with his friend Graham Young instead of going to school dinner.

Williams was not what one could call a brilliant boy, and the penny did not drop. Later in the year he shared food or drink with his chum and the same thing occurred. On one occasion the two boys went for a Saturday outing to the Zoo. Although Williams provided the packed lunch, Graham brought two bottles of lemonade, one of which he handed to his friend and the other he kept for his own use. On the way home the two boys had barely reached the Underground in Finchley Road when Williams was violently sick. He spent the next few days in bed with stomach pains and his family called the doctor, but he was unable to pin-point the cause, even when the boy began to have severe cramp in his arms and legs and blinding headaches. Eventually the patient was admitted to Willesden Hospital, where migraine was diagnosed and he was prescribed tablets.

After his hospitalization Williams recovered and went home, and so long as he did not return to school he remained free of symptoms. But after resuming his schooling he was to experience a return of his disabling illness, on and off, for the next several months. Since school dinners did not affect any of the other boys in this way, food poisoning was ruled out, and it was thought that Williams must be allergic to one or more of the foods used. He therefore began to take packed lunches made up at home on a regular basis, in an effort to avoid whatever food it was that was affecting him. Alas! – it was not realized that this would make him even more likely to be used as a guinea-pig by his friend Graham Young for his 'experiments' either by swapping sandwiches or by bringing bottles of squash. Williams continued to suffer.

At about this time Molly Young found a bottle of antimony in her stepson's room, clearly marked 'Poison'. He was forbidden to bring any more noxious substances into the house and to confine his experiments to those which employed innocuous compounds. Molly went to see Geoffrey Reis and told him in no uncertain terms to stop selling poisons to her stepson. Even then, no one connected the intermittent sickness of Williams to his friend's 'experiments' – and the ban on Geoffrey Reis's shop being his supply depot had little effect: he simply obtained them elsewhere.

Another Neasden chemist, Edgar Davies, was now used as the main source of poisons by the youthful purveyor of death to cats and mice and agonizing illness to his fellow humans. Soon after Molly Young had vetoed Geoffrey Reis's shop, she became ill herself with the identical symptoms that beset Williams. Towards the end of 1961 she had two severe attacks, but incredibly she thought it to be only a bout of gastric flu and afterwards gave it no more thought. Then her husband, Fred Young, came down with two similar attacks. Graham's sister Winifred was taken ill suddenly on her way to meet her boyfriend for an evening at the cinema. The family thought that there must be a 'bug' going around. There was a good deal of meticulous hand-washing and careful boiling of cutlery and crockery, but the sickness continued.

One morning Winifred thought that her cup of tea tasted 'a bit peculiar' and told Molly. They thought that perhaps it had been a cup in which Molly had mixed her shampoo and forgotten to wash. They thought no more of it, but on her way to her office job Winifred began to feel most peculiar herself. Dizziness assailed her; the other passengers on the Underground train seemed first to recede, then to lunge towards her. She could not focus properly. She was helped off the train and managed to get to her office near Tottenham Court Road, but she found work impossible as she could not see to take shorthand or to type. A colleague took her to the Middlesex Hospital, where she spent the rest of the day undergoing tests. A doctor eventually diagnosed belladonna poisoning.

Winifred was angry when she arrived home – angry at having lost a day at work and angry with her brother whom she openly accused of being careless with his chemicals. His father, reluctant to believe that his thirteen-year-old son was defying him after his chemicals had been banned from the house, knew that Graham had been in the habit of conducting his experiments in a disused allotment shed on a council site a few hundred yards along the road. Instead of searching his son's room, he searched the rest of the house and sent Graham to bed early!

Belladonna is a derivative of the deadly nightshade plant and was purchased by Graham in the form of atropine, along with further supplies of antimony, arsenic, digitalis, aconitine and thallium, from the Neasden chemist he now patronized. Thallium was eventually to become his favourite poison. And while his family were searching the kitchen, the living-room and other parts of the house and garden, Graham had secreted in his room enough poisons of various kinds to kill 300 people.

Molly Young, quite suddenly, started to look much older. She lost weight and developed a stoop like an old woman. She constantly complained of stomach and back pains, and tingling in her arms and legs. She thought it might have originated from a bus accident in the late summer of 1961 when the seat in which she was travelling was ripped from its moorings during the crash, catapulting her outwards and upwards so that she hit her head violently on the roof.

On Easter Saturday, 21 April 1962, Molly awakened feeling, as she put it, 'jolly grotty'. She had a stiff neck, tingling in her hands and feet, and back pains. Still, she decided to nip out to the shops, so that the family would not be short of bread and other basic necessities over the Easter holiday when the shops would be closed. When she got home she was feeling much worse, and went out into the garden to get a bit of fresh air. When her husband returned home from the pub where he had his usual Saturday lunchtime pint, he saw his wife writhing in agony on the lawn garden seat. Graham, he was astonished to find, was sitting at the window in the house staring out at her. He had made no move to go and see what was wrong or to offer any assistance – not even the glass of lemonade he was usually so prompt to offer. Still, before she went out he had made her a cup of tea …

The following morning Molly was no better and Fred, her husband, took her to see Dr Wills, the family's GP, who insisted that she be admitted to Willesden Hospital and kept in for observation. By late afternoon that day, even before the doctors had been able to discover what was wrong with her, she had died. The cause of death was attributed to the delayed effects of the bus accident, and an inquest was considered unnecessary.

Fred Young was shattered; Winifred was stunned. Graham suggested that his stepmother should be cremated – so much more hygienic than burial, he argued. He harped on this theme so much that his family was deeply shocked, and his father told him tersely to shut up. At the funeral, Graham said not a word; his attention was riveted on watching the evidence of his crime going up in smoke – literally as well as metaphorically. The police could never charge him, he gloated to himself, with a perfect murder all evidence of which had been destroyed ...

At the traditional family gathering after the funeral, Graham continued to maintain a discreet silence, while all around him family, friends and neighbours commented on how dreadful it was for a fourteen-year-old boy to be left motherless. For, in effect, Molly *had* been his mother – his real mother had died of tuberculosis when he was only a three-month-old baby. He nodded politely when spoken to, but did not join in the conversation. It was a minor diversion, therefore, when Molly's brother-in-law, Graham's Uncle John, began to vomit violently after eating a ham sandwich and mustard pickles.

Everyone had been eating the sandwiches, but only Uncle John partook of the mustard pickles. Lacing these with antimony had been little more than a practical joke. But now Graham decided that the time had come to choose the next guinea-pig – his father Fred. It would be logical, he thought, if Fred Young should die within weeks of his wife's death, his end hastened by the shock. So Graham got down to the serious business of working out how best to achieve this end. After having fed Molly antimony in sustained non-fatal quantities for more than a year, he suddenly realized that she had probably built up a resistance to the poison, and on 20 April, the night before she died, he doctored her supper with twenty grains of thallium – enough to kill a dozen people.

While his wife was alive Fred used to come home to lunch as he preferred her cooking to the fare dished out at his works' canteen. Now that she was gone, he still came home, but opened cans and knocked up so-called 'ready meals' as he was no great shakes as a cook. On one occasion he opened a can of corned beef and went out to buy some chips to put with it, and opened a can of pineapple for dessert. An hour after his return to work in the afternoon, he felt so ill that, in his own words, 'I thought I was going to die'. He had never known stomach pains or vomiting like it. The attack passed off, and by the evening he felt himself again. The works' nurse thought it was something he had eaten and sent him home early, but he recovered fairly quickly and was able to go in to work the next day.

A few weeks later Fred had another attack, accompanied by severe diarrhoea. The stomach pains were excruciating, and Winifred called Dr Wills, who told him to come to the surgery the next morning if he did not improve after taking the tablets he prescribed. In the surgery he collapsed and was rushed into hospital by ambulance. The astonishment and consternation of the family can be better conjectured than described when the doctors told them that Fred's condition was consistent with poisoning, either by antimony or arsenic. And while the horrified family gathered round the patient's bedside, Graham was animatedly explaining to the doctors how they could distinguish between the presenting symptoms of the two poisons, completely absorbed in his subject.

The next day, antimony poisoning was confirmed, and Fred Young was told that one more dose would have killed him. He had a good chance of recovery, but his liver had been permanently damaged. At school, Graham told his friends that his father was now ill in hospital just a few weeks after his stepmother's death. Clive Creager was convinced that Graham had poisoned both of them, and told his parents of his suspicions, but they scoffed at the idea and told him he had been reading to many horror comics. In the end, it was Graham's science master who decided to take action.

Having encouraged the boy to make full use of the science laboratory, he had steadily become more and more perturbed at the kind of experiments his student was conducting, spending hours meticulously analysing poisons and recording his conclusions in a notebook. One evening after school he decided to take a look at Graham's notebook and opened Graham's desk. Not only did he find the notebook but also, to his surprise, bottles containing deadly poisons, none of which could be legally obtained by anyone under seventeen (Graham was still only fourteen at the time). He also found drawings and poems on various macabre themes, including poisonings and poisoners. Remembering Christopher Williams and his mysterious illness, the science teacher decided to confide his growing suspicions in the headmaster. They decided that it would be premature to go to the police, but arranged for a psychiatrist to interview him in the guise of being a 'careers officer' and hoped that they themselves would be let off the hook by Graham warming to his favourite subject during the interview and incriminating himself. Their hope was to be realized.

Graham, unable to resist such an opportunity of giving a dazzling display of his knowledge, excelled himself at discoursing on the technicalities of toxicology and his controlled experiments in the science laboratory. He was able to back this up with an account of his academic record, with his position as top of his class in chemistry, physics and mathematics, adding with a disarmingly modest touch the admission that his geometry could do with a bit of brushing up. The 'careers officer' told him that he was bright enough to aim for a place at university after leaving school, reading chemistry. Graham went home in a daze of good feeling, convinced that a brilliant career lay before him – if only he played his cards right and didn't become careless. What he did not know was that the 'careers officer' had gone straight to the police. Graham had given away far more than he had been aware of in his euphoric enthusiasm.

The next day, 21 May, Detective Inspector Edward Crabbe called at the family home. In Graham's room he found varying quantities of deadly poisons as well as a number of books on poisons and poisoners. As soon as Graham returned from school, Detective Inspector Crabbe told the boy to turn out his pockets, and a phial of antimony and two small bottles of thallium were found among the usual schoolboy odds and ends. The poisons were removed to be sent for analysis, and Graham was taken to Harlesden police station. All night he was interrogated by a team of officers, and he denied everything. But the following day he changed his mind, and decided to make a full confession, after which he was charged with poisoning Christopher Williams, Fred Young and Winifred Young, and remanded in custody for trial at the Old Bailey.

The family was horrified and shocked. How could a thirteen-year-old boy have been systematically poisoning his own family? They refused to believe it. Even the notion that crockery or food had been inadvertently contaminated during his 'experiments' was alien to them. The whole idea frightened them. Williams was his closest friend; the other two victims mentioned in the indictment were his own father and his sister. Impossible! There are none so blind as those who will not see. After all, Graham never showed any animosity towards either his friend or his family except for the odd one or two incidents which could happen in any family after a ticking-off.

What the family did not realize was that Graham had the detached objectivity of the scientific researcher. He chose the victims simply because they were close at hand and he could monitor their reactions to his experiments. He could observe and note the results of his researches with scientific precision. When he watched a victim's agony, it was not with a sadistic pleasure; it was merely a detached observation, entirely devoid of feeling.

On July 6 he came before Mr Justice Melford Stevenson at the Old Bailey. At his trial he spoke only once, to plead guilty to all three counts. Mr E.J.P. Cussens, prosecuting, pointed out that for some considerable time the boy had been buying dangerous poisons from chemists' shops despite his being under the legal age to do so and he strongly criticized the chemists for having allowed a child to bamboozle them into selling him substances which could kill. It was clear, Mr Cussens said, that Young had a vast knowledge of poisons, but this was no excuse.

Although in his full confession Young admitted having administered antimony to his stepmother over a protracted period, it was pointed out at the trial that the death certificate stated her death to have derived from other causes, namely, the after-effects of a bus crash. Young had omitted in his confession to mention the fatal dose of thallium he had given her the night before she died. It is not known whether he deliberately omitted this or whether it slipped his mind. Perhaps the former is the more likely, since it is in keeping with the sense of power he had achieved by having committed what he considered to be the perfect murder.

Under Section Sixty-six of the Mental Health Act, 1959, the judge committed Young to Broadmoor, adding a restriction order that he must not be released for fifteen years without the authority of the Home Secretary.

Fred Young, released from hospital, brooded about 'that bloody boy and what he'd been getting up to' and refused to visit him. He sold the family house in North London and moved to Sheerness in Kent with his sister and brother-in-law. They, together with Graham's sister Winifred, made the trip to Berkshire whenever they could. Winifred had by now married Dennis Shannon, the boyfriend she had arranged to meet for an evening at the cinema on the night she was taken ill, and was expecting their first child. One of Graham's uncles who visited him fairly often because he lived much nearer remembers Graham pestering him for an unending supply of boxes of matches, until other members of the family mentioned that they had never known Graham to smoke, and it was then that he realized that the poisonous substance phosphorus could be obtained if one had a sufficient quantity of matches. Was he up to his tricks again and slipping something into other patients' tea?

Less than a month after Young had been admitted to Broadmoor, there was a sudden death. John Berridge, a twenty-three-year-old former soldier who had been sent to Broadmoor after shooting both his parents, collapsed in convulsions and quickly died in Ward Three, Block Four on 6 August 1962. A post-mortem was conducted and this showed that he had died from cyanide poisoning. He was not considered to be suicidal, and since no cyanide in any form was kept in the institution the death of the patient was a complete mystery. It was unlikely that anyone could have smuggled cyanide in, but then someone pointed out that the farmland adjoining the boundary fences was planted with a profusion of laurel bushes. From these, an expert with sufficient know-how would be able to distil enough cyanide to kill the entire Broadmoor population.

Young was naturally the prime suspect, and he appeared to revel in his notoriety and seized the opportunity of showing off his knowledge, describing in accurate and minute detail how cyanide can be extracted from the leaves of the common laurel. However, the authorities were not convinced that Young had anything to do with it, and the case was marked unsolved.

Young was regarded with suspicion, however, by many of his fellow-patients, and even some of the nurses thought that there might have been some cause for concern. It became a common joke for nurses to tell patients who were causing trouble 'I'll let Graham make your tea for you if you don't behave yourself!' Young made no secret of the fact that he enjoyed this shaft of limelight in such an unlikely setting, and he would talk like a medical textbook at every opportunity to compound the situation. Plans had previously been afoot to transfer him to a ward where he would have had more freedom, but these were hastily shelved and he remained in Ward One of the admission block indefinitely. With the prospect of a long stay in the institution, he decorated his room, number Five, with pictures of Nazi leaders, and painted skulls and crossbones on the containers provided for his tea, sugar and so on, often erasing the real names for the products and substituting complicated chemical formulae – invariably of poisons.

He had unrestricted access to books of all kinds in both the libraries which served the institution – its own library and the visiting mobile library. He was able to read such books as *The Rise and Fall of the Third Reich*, Bram Stoker's *Dracula* and Dennis Wheatley's black magic novels, as well as the most abstruse textbooks of medicine, forensic pathology, toxicology, chemistry and physics. He also learned German, and developed a taste for Wagner. He was allowed to attend football and cricket matches on the playing field, but showed no inclination to join in. During handicraft classes he made wooden and metal swastikas, and would always wear one or other of them on a chain around his neck.

Eventually, after a year of settling in which had its difficult times, he began to blend in more smoothly with the community, and some of the nurses even trusted him to make their coffee – until one day when he laced it with Harpic. At this time he was reading *The Scourge of the Swastika* and a study of Haigh, the acid bath murderer. Things continued in this vein until the appropriate time came for him to make his first application to the review tribunal for his release. His family was requested to attend the tribunal, which consisted of a number of doctors and psychiatrists. His father voiced the opinion that he should never be released, and none of his family was willing to offer him a home if he were released. The application was rejected.

Not unnaturally Graham was bitterly disappointed, and this escalated to an intense resentment. Not long afterwards a nurse noticed that a packet of Manger's sugar soap, used for cleaning the washbasins in the admission block, was missing from its normal place and a search was instituted. The newly filled tea urn was intercepted at the start of the tea trolley's round; analysis showed that the entire contents of the packet of the caustic substance had been poured into it.

The incident was to be the last of its kind Young would perpetrate while in Broadmoor. This was not because he did not wish to do so but purely as a cunning ploy to induce the staff to think he had 'reformed' and was no longer interested in poisoning anybody, because he knew that if his next application for release were to stand any chance of success then he must be on his best behaviour. This self-restraint made him very moody, and he would often go for days without talking to anyone. But, in contrast, he became more forthcoming with the psychiatrists who had been trying, often unsuccessfully, to fathom the strange obsessions of this boy who loved heavy metal poisons as a normal boy would love dogs or football.

Eventually, at the end of his fifth year, during which his psychiatrists had seen the progress of his studies and suggested that he could seriously think about university after his release, he was transferred to Block Two, which offered more freedom within the hospital buildings and grounds. His good behaviour could not now be faulted. Letters he wrote to his family and friends emphasized the fact that he considered it very unlikely that he would have to remain in Broadmoor for fifteen years. He felt this so strongly that he even made applications for employment on the outside in anticipation of his release. These included an application for a job with a police forensic science laboratory, which was rejected out of hand. He also applied to join the training scheme of the Pharmaceutical Society, which was also, predictably, refused.

In June 1970 Graham's psychiatrists reported to the Home Office that he 'was no longer a danger to others' and that 'profound changes had taken place' in response to treatment. 'He is no longer obsessed with poisons,' wrote one doctor. They obviously had not heard Graham say to a nurse, 'When I get out, I'm going to kill one person for every year I've spent in this place.' Another nurse was later to recall: 'We were all against Graham's release. He made no secret of the fact that he intended to poison again. Indeed, he enjoyed boasting about his ambition to go down in history as the most famous poisoner since Crippen.'

The nurses did not report these conversations to the authorities but treated them as just examples of Graham's macabre idea of a joke, of less significance than pouring Harpic or caustic cleaning powder into the tea. So it was in ignorance of these avowals that a well-meaning but ill-advised recommendation for Graham's release was put forward by the doctors, ratified by Broadmoor's superintendent, to the Home Office. The response was to allow him a weekend visit to his family on licence. Winifred, his sister, decided to forgive him and let bygones be bygones. It was a mental aberration of youth, she believed. With young children in the house, she knew that she was taking a calculated risk, but such is the power of family love. This love was not, however, shared by Graham's other relatives, who were dismayed and appalled that he should be allowed the freedom of the outside world, even if only from Friday to Sunday.

Nothing untoward occurred during his first taste of freedom for so many years. Whether or not he harboured any latent desire to slip something into his sister's tea or the baby's bottle, he knew that if he were to regain his final freedom he must not blot his copybook. His ploy worked; later that year he was allowed a week's leave, again staying with Winifred.

Graham spent a pleasant week with his sister and brother-in-law, enjoying normal activities, visiting the pub for a beer, taking the dog for a walk and so on. Graham rarely mentioned poisons or chemistry, although he did tend to dominate the conversation with his current subject of study, the First World War. All in all, the week of trial was a success, and Winifred and her husband gave the Broadmoor authorities a favourable report. It was arranged that Graham would spend Christmas with them, and that time, too, passed without incident, although Winifred and Dennis did notice that Graham was smoking rather heavily and drinking more than was good for him. They ascribed this to 'making up for lost time' after the restrictions imposed by Broadmoor: smoking was allowed only in strict moderation, and alcohol of any kind, even beer, was forbidden.

The movement towards Graham's release now gathered momentum, and the Home Office order was signed early in 1971. Three conditions were imposed: he must reside at a fixed address, he must be supervised by the probation service, and he must attend a psychiatric out-patient clinic on a regular basis. After eight years, he was to be free at last. Several doctors, as well as quite a few of the nursing staff, had grave misgivings; but they could not overrule a Home Office directive. Even with the restrictions imposed, it was a bit like throwing a non-swimmer into the deep end with the command 'Swim!'

On Thursday, 4 February 1971, Graham Young rejoiced as the gates of Broadmoor closed behind him. He had arranged to join a Government training centre in Slough, which would start the following Monday. Heading for his sister's home in Hemel Hempstead, he greeted her with a salutation that had an ominous ring: 'Hi! Guess who? It's your friendly neighbourhood Frankenstein again!' Winifred forced a laugh and mildly ticked him off. 'Don't talk like that!' she said. He spent the four days before starting his new training programme visiting the pub with his brother-in-law and launching into lengthy discourses on the First World War, Hitler's policies, the British policy in

Ulster and terrorism generally. The continual arguments became wearisome after a while, and Graham was told to 'give over', but at least it was better than continually talking about chemicals and poisons, his relatives agreed. Weighty tomes on these subjects soon found their way into his room from the local public library, but Winifred stifled her concern when Graham explained that these were needed for his studies to get him into university in due course.

Within days of starting at the centre where he was training to acquire the skills needed for a storekeeper's job, Graham struck up a friendship with another trainee, thirty-four-year-old Trevor Sparkes, who had arrived two weeks earlier and had a room in town. The two visited a pub called the Grapes in Slough; both were dedicated beer men. On occasions, they would retire to Sparkes's room with a bottle of wine, provided by Young, and spend hours discussing animatedly and at length politics, history, war, music, medicine and, inevitably, chemistry. Sparkes was not very conversant with this latter subject, his main interest being football. He was a keen amateur footballer. Football, and sport generally, left Young cold, but this somewhat ill-matched couple were held together by the magnetism of Young's enthusiasm for argument and discussion, and the pleasures of Bacchus.

A week after Young's arrival at the centre, Sparkes had been playing on the pitch of his amateur club when he was seized by a bout of sharp abdominal pains. He consulted his GP, who could find nothing seriously wrong. The pains continued, and he vomited while at work one afternoon. He was sent home from the centre and told to go back to his doctor. Despite medication, the vomiting continued and he was also tormented by pains in the groin, chronic diarrhoea, and 'pins and needles' in the legs. His face began to swell, and he was admitted to hospital. A stomach infection was diagnosed and he was treated with antibiotics and antacid tablets. The vomiting stopped, the pains eased, and he returned to the centre.

A week or so later the pains returned, although he had no vomiting or diarrhoea. On the football pitch that Saturday he suddenly found his legs going out of control, with tingling and numbness in alternating spasms from his thighs to his toes. Finally he had to leave the pitch. He has never played football since.

In the months that followed, Sparkes had several recurrences of the abdominal pains, vomiting and diarrhoea, and was examined by no fewer than seven doctors and consultants, including physicians at Queen Elizabeth II Hospital in Welwyn Garden City, his home town. It seemed that not even the specialists could discern what was actually wrong, for the patient was variously diagnosed as having a stomach infection, a kidney infection, a urinary infection, a bowel infection – or, perhaps, they were all partially right, since heavy metal poisons affect the whole system ...

Sparkes left the centre and returned home for good, and meanwhile what of our friendly neighbourhood Frankenstein? He was staying for weekends with an aunt and uncle in London from time to time in order to provide a convenient cover for his visits to John Bell and Croyden, the famous Wigmore Street chemists, where he purchased a number of Schedule I (restricted) poisons on a forged letter of authority typed on a college's printed heading. It is not known how he obtained this, but for a young man who had been able to obtain restricted poisons as a twelve-year-old boy, obtaining college headed paper and forging a letter of authority must have been very small beer indeed.

Early in April 1971 a vacancy for a storekeeper was advertised by a firm called Hadland's in the village of Bovingdon, near Hemel Hempstead, which manufactured high-grade optical and photographic apparatus. Young made an application for this job, sponsored by the training centre. On the application form he wrote: 'I have studied organic and inorganic chemistry, pharmacology and toxicology for ten years, and I therefore have some knowledge of chemicals and their usage.' Young was fully aware that thallium, which was now his favourite poison even preferred to antimony, is used mainly as an industrial chemical by the makers of optical lenses with a high refractive index – exactly the kind of work carried out by Hadland's. The great irony, however, was that no thallium at all was stocked by Hadland's and Young had to travel to London – a fifty-mile round trip – to purchase it!

Another very curious facet of this job application was

that any such application had to be approved by the Broadmoor authorities, and it seemed that Broadmoor's officer responsible for the approval of the application was content for Young to obtain a job in a photographic and optical equipment laboratory knowing that he was a convicted poisoner who had used thallium!

The centre was obliged to inform a prospective employer that Young had undergone treatment in a mental hospital, but not to specify that it had been Broadmoor. Young, asked about this, said that he had had a nervous breakdown of lengthy duration, and the remainder of the time he had spent studying for a degree in chemistry. The managing director of Hadland's, Godfrey Foster, was perfectly satisfied with this explanation, and offered the enthusiastic young man the job.

Winifred had agreed to let her brother stay with her for as long as he needed to settle into his new life. But the probation service liked to encourage parolees to aim for independence of family ties and to find a place of their own, while still maintaining close supportive links with their families by regular visits, family outings and the like. So Young looked around for a place of his own in Hemel Hempstead, and eventually found a spacious room in Maynard's Road, in a semi-detached house owned by a Pakistani family, at a rent of four pounds weekly. His room was well-supplied with built-in cupboards, the shelves in which soon became lined with a veritable repository of blue, green and brown bottles, which his friends called 'the apothecary's shop'. Other shelves housed his growing collection of books, mainly heavy treatises on toxicology, pharmacology, medical jurisprudence and chemistry – his university study textbooks, he told his friends. To these were added books borrowed from the public library, which conveniently was just across the road. Posters of his Nazi war heroes decorated the walls, along with swastikas which he had carved in wood or wrought in metal in the craft workshops of Broadmoor.

Young commenced work at Hadland's on 10 May 1971 as a £24-a-week storekeeper. His new work-mates were a cheerful group who quickly befriended him, though they found him very unpredictable and sometimes moody.

One day he would brightly join in the banter, while
another would see him withdrawn and barely speaking to
anyone. He usually spent the morning and afternoon
tea-breaks sitting alone reading, and his work-mates
observed that his books were invariably war, Nazism,
famous murderers, or chemistry. He only really came alive
when he engaged someone in a heated discussion on one
of his pet topics: chemistry or politics. His favourite topic
was Hitler. One of his work-mates, Bob Egle, fifty-nine,
was a Dunkirk veteran, and Young would badger him at
every opportunity to tell him about his wartime
experiences.

At other times, though, Young was observed to be
absent-minded, distant and even curt. He frequently
seemed to be far away, carrying out his duties mechani-
cally while his mind was absorbed in his own private
fantasies. He had to check in stock, enter it into a book,
pack goods outwards for distribution and enter them into
a different book; all this required concentration. So from
time to time older members of the staff gave him a verbal
prod back to reality. They did not want misrouted goods
or incorrect entries in the daybooks. Young did not take
kindly to reproof, and would often go off in a huff if
spoken to in this way.

About a month after Young had joined Hadland's, Bob
Egle was suddenly taken ill. He was sent home with acute
stomach pains and severe diarrhoea. He was ill over the
weekend and stayed in bed, but felt sufficiently recovered
on Monday, 7 June, to return to his job as stores
supervisor.

The following day Ron Hewitt, another stores department employee, was taken ill after drinking a cup of tea
which he had asked Young to bring him. Crippling
stomach pains were accompanied by vomiting and
diarrhoea, and there was a burning sensation at the back
of his throat. He, too, was sent home. The following day
the symptoms still persisted and his GP was called in, who
diagnosed food poisoning. He had to spend the rest of the
week in bed. The vomiting, stomach pains and diarrhoea
continued, and the burning in his throat became worse. By
Monday he felt well enough to return to work, but he did
not feel really fit – 'still a bit dodgy', as he told his

colleagues. Over the next few weeks he had a further dozen or so bouts of the same symptoms, so that he was on and off work, as he put it, 'like a bloody yo-yo'.

Bob Egle was still not feeling as well as he had been before his illness, and he felt that this was as good a time as any to take his annual family holiday, this time at Yarmouth. A couple of days before he was due to return, Graham Young took one of his periodic trips to London, on Friday night, 25 June, after finishing work. He stayed with his aunt and uncle, and on the Saturday bought twenty-five grams of thallium in John Bell and Croyden's. He always signed for the poisons in the name of 'M.E. Evans', giving an address in Willesden, just as he had done as a boy. By Sunday he was back in his bedsitter replenishing the somewhat depleted stocks in his private laboratory.

Unlike many other poisons, thallium is completely tasteless, colourless and odourless, so, from the poisoner's point of view, it has the advantage that it can be administered to a victim in food or drink without the person being aware that he or she is being poisoned. Before Young used it, thallium had never before been employed by a poisoner in Britain.

Bob Egle returned to work on the Monday from his seaside holiday, feeling perfectly well. Naturally he attributed this to the sea air, rather than to the absence of thallium in his tea. Unfortunately for poor Bob, Young was determined to continue using him as the most convenient guinea-pig for his experiments, purely because, since they worked together all the time, he could monitor his reactions to the varying doses. After all, it was much more convenient than choosing a subject who worked at the opposite end of the building. Not that he would have jibbed at that if he had to.

Young did not waste any time. The very next day after Bob's return to work, he felt so ill that he had to go straight home. He told his wife that his fingers had gone numb at the ends. She gave him what must have been his first unadulterated cup of tea for two days and he lay on the sofa until dinner-time, but he did not want any food. Later the same evening his wife suggested that a walk in the fresh air might do him good, so they started out along the road towards the stables where their daughter kept her pony. But they never got that far; Bob started staggering about like a drunk. His wife took him back home and he went to bed.

The next morning Bob told his wife that his feet had gone numb as well as his fingers, and he had shooting pain in his back which was not relieved by a hot-water bottle or aspirin. His wife called their doctor, who gave him some tablets, but every time he took them he vomited. He stayed in bed, unable to resume work, and with the pains increasing the doctor was called in again. He diagnosed peripheral neuritis and admitted Bob to hospital for tests.

In the ambulance which took him to the West Hertfordshire Hospital in Hemel Hempstead, his back pain was so intense that he was writhing in agony. The following day he was transferred to the intensive care unit in St Albans' City Hospital, twelve miles from Hemel Hempstead. His condition deteriorated from day to day, the paralysis which had commenced in his fingertips spreading throughout his entire body. He could hear what was said to him, but could not reply. His condition worsened, and on 7 July he died. His family was shattered.

Graham Young had appeared to show a great deal of concern for Bob. Every day he would badger his boss with questions about Bob's progress, and even called the hospital several times. The nurses who took his calls noted that when told he could not speak to one of the doctors who was treating the patient, he seemed to become quite annoyed.

Bob Egle's death shook the seventy-five members of Hadland's staff. Ron Hewitt left two days later, and Young was promoted to take over his job. He appeared to enjoy being in charge of the stores since the demise of the supervisor and Ron's leaving. Ron had been Bob's assistant and Young's immediate superior. No one at Hadland's saw any reason to connect Bob's sudden death with the mysterious illness which had racked Ron Hewitt.

At the post-mortem on Bob Egle, death was certified as being due to broncho-pneumonia associated with a little-known form of polyneuritis called Guillaume-Barré's syndrome. An inquest was deemed unnecessary. The cremation service was arranged for the following Monday, and Godfrey Foster, as managing director, attended the funeral to represent Hadland's. He took Young with him to represent the department of which Bob had been head and who was now, in effect, acting head of stores. On the way to the cremation service at Amersham, Young talked to Foster incessantly about polyneuritis, Guillaume-Barré's syndrome and the treatment currently in use for these conditions. Foster later was to state that he was 'absolutely amazed at Young's knowledge of medicine', though he could not remember 'all the long words he had used', which had gone right over his head. After the service Young continued to discuss the hypothetical causes of Egle's death and the nature of his illness. And Foster continued to be amazed. 'You'd have thought you were talking to a doctor, and a specialist at that,' he said. 'You'd never have thought he was a storekeeper. He was in the wrong job. But he had told me he was studying and hoped to go to university later.'

For the next couple of months life at Hadland's was uneventful. Young, now in full charge of stores, tended to show off his authority, and he had certainly become much more outgoing since the death of Egle. He continually raised that subject, even when it was made clear to him that no one else really wanted to talk about it, and he still discussed Hitler, the war, chemistry and his other obsessions *ad nauseam*. Those who did not want to listen simply avoided him. But others were quick to notice some of his 'weird habits' such as working in the dark and, in particular, his obvious enjoyment in killing insects with a fly spray and watching them die. But no one twigged anything of the macabre compulsions which were dominating his life. A member of staff named Fred Biggs, who was a keen gardener, asked his advice on destroying the pests which were causing havoc in his garden. Young brought some nicotine which he offered to give Biggs to kill the pests, even offering to come and do the job himself. Biggs refused both offers. Young walked off with a look of obvious annoyance on his face. When Biggs had occasion to advise Young on some ideas for improving the system in the stores, Young retorted, 'Why should I do what you tell me to do? You're not my boss. Anyway, I gave you some good advice for your gardening problem and you don't even want to know, although it will not cost you a penny.' He stalked off in a huff.

The calm at Hadlands was rudely shattered in September, when Fred Biggs suddenly started vomiting and complaining of sharp stabbing stomach pains. He was due to start his holiday that weekend which he managed to do on Sunday, instead of the intended Saturday, when the symptoms had abated.

On Monday, 20 September, the firm's import-export manager, Peter Buck, had what he described as a 'bilious attack' shortly after having a cup of tea with Young and David Tilson, one of the clerks. A headache, feelings of nausea and tingling in the fingers preceded the vomiting. David Tilson took him home in his car. The following day he was back at work feeling little the worse, and he was not, as far as is known, to have any repetition of the attack at any later date.

Tilson was the next member of the staff to suffer the by now all too familiar symptoms, about three weeks later. On Friday, 8 October, he started to feel a bit queasy after the morning tea-break. However, he managed to keep going and continue working. The next day at home he started to feel pins and needles in his feet. These feelings persisted throughout the night and into Sunday, by which time his legs had become completely numb. On Monday he was no better, and struggled to his doctor's surgery with the aid of a stick. As the day progressed the numbness wore off but was replaced by shooting pains in his legs. He managed to get to work on Tuesday, although his legs were stiff, but the shooting pains had gone.

On the Friday Young was being assisted in the stores by Jethro Batt, a clerk who had been assigned to help him when orders were particularly plentiful. Young's conversation, as usual, was rather morbid, and Batt told him playfully to 'put a sock in it' and asked him whether he did not in fact have more pleasant things to talk about. 'Tell you what,' Young replied, 'I'll make us both a cup of coffee. Make a change from tea.' Unfortunately for Jethro Batt, one of the constituents of Young's coffee was the same as that of Young's tea. Batt rushed to the toilets twenty minutes later to be violently sick. He decided to call it a day, as he was feeling distinctly 'dodgy'. As by this time it was almost time to clock off, Batt offered Young a lift home in his car.

Over that weekend Batt did not vomit but he started having pains in his legs which became increasingly severe. David Tilson, meanwhile, was not feeling much better. The pains in his legs had not returned, but he was feeling pins and needles in his feet once again. Monday morning saw both men in their respective doctors' surgeries; Batt's legs had gone numb and the pains had moved up to his stomach, while Tilson complained of chest and stomach pains and difficulty in breathing, stiff joints and tingling in the feet. The two doctors were completely mystified.

The next day Tilson was much worse and was admitted to St. Albans' City Hospital for tests. Vomiting returned, and his hair began to fall out. Batt did not go into hospital but stayed at home, in bed. He had agonizing leg pains as well as chest and stomach spasms.

Back at Hadland's, Mrs Diana Smart, a wiring department worker who occasionally helped out in stores, had a cup of coffee with Young, who now had to manage his department single-handed until such time as a permanent assistant could be appointed. Soon afterwards she developed identical symptoms to those which had been plaguing her colleagues. She was taken home.

Tilson remained in hospital until 28 October. Although not completely recovered, his condition was no longer deteriorating, and he wanted to go home. However, when he climbed stairs or even walked more than a few steps, his pulse and heart began to quicken to an alarming rate. His hair began to fall out, and he felt so bad that he stayed in bed. Just four days after his discharge he was readmitted. Doctors were completely baffled by his symptoms. Batt, too, was admitted to hospital on 5 November. The intense and agonizing pains he was suffering were making him suicidal and he had to be kept under sedation. He had lost most of his hair, and he could not get out of bed unaided because his toes had gone rigid.

Things were very difficult at Hadland's with Tilson, Batt and Mrs Smart off sick, and no replacement yet found for Bob Egle; Hewitt had left, and Graham Young was left holding the fort in his department, which was overworked and understaffed – a matter on which Young was not slow to complain. Biggs was still on holiday. Staff were allocated to help out on a voluntary overtime basis, and for the first time the firm was going to have to work on Saturdays in order to catch up on the backlog of orders. Mrs Bartlett, the tea lady, would be unable to come in owing to unavoidable Saturday commitments, so Graham arranged with her to let him have the key to the cupboard in which the supplies of tea and coffee were kept. On this first occasion the managing director, Godfrey Foster, came along to see how everyone was managing and when he reached the stores Young, naturally enough, offered him a cup of tea, but it so happened that Mr Foster did not want one: probably a good thing!

The following Saturday Fred Biggs was there as he had returned from his holiday. Everyone told him how well he was looking and said they wished it were the time for *their* holidays. That night Biggs and his wife went out for a night on the town in London. This was to celebrate his wife's birthday which was on the following Tuesday but they thought Saturday a better time than in the middle of the working week. Fred Biggs was not to know that only two days after his wife's birthday he would be in hospital, as a result of drinking tea that Young had made.

He enjoyed his night out and felt nothing wrong until Sunday, when he began to feel just generally unwell. He did not ascribe this to over-indulgence in alcohol, because he was a very moderate drinker by any standards, even on birthdays. He still felt unwell and visited his GP on Monday as he did not feel up to going in to work. By Tuesday he had developed acute chest pains and had difficulty in walking, and by Wednesday he could not get out of bed. On Thursday, 4 November, he was admitted to the West Hertfordshire Hospital in Hemel Hempstead.

By now Godfrey Foster, as managing director, was so concerned at the spate of serious illness that beset his firm that he decided to call in outside help. He asked Dr Robert Hynd, the Medical Officer of Health for the district, to investigate. The illness had received the local name of the 'Bovingdon bug', and the two most popular theories were either that the water was contaminated or that recent radioactive work in a disused Government airfield was at fault. The former theory was the more popular, because it had been noticed that all the attacks followed the imbibing of tea or coffee on the firm's premises. How the water had become contaminated, they theorized, was anybody's guess, but chemicals used in the factory were not ruled out.

Mrs Smart, who had by now returned to work, voiced her view that Graham Young, because he never suffered any of the attacks, was a 'virus carrier' who himself had immunity. This opinion made her very unpopular with Young, and it was no coincidence that she had another attack later that same day, after she had been unwise enough to drink a cup of coffee made with the allegedly 'contaminated' water. She was off work for a week.

Young made a great show of concern for his colleagues. He pestered the managing director's secretary for news of their progress, nipping in and out of her office whenever Mr Foster was engaged elsewhere. Fortunately he did not offer her a cup of tea or coffee when he did so. The day after Fred Biggs was taken to hospital he telephoned Mrs Biggs at home to ask after Fred, and was told that the doctors were unable to pin-point what was wrong. Young then asked her if he could visit him, but was told that only family visitors were allowed. Young, not to be deterred, then rang the hospital, but was puzzled when he was informed that they had no patient there named Fred Biggs. Only later did he discover that this was because Biggs had been transferred to the Whittington Hospital at Archway in London for specialists to examine him.

On this day, Thursday, 11 November, Dr Robert Hynd visited Hadland's with a team of doctors and members of the Department of Factory Inspectors. They spent all day at the works and made an exhaustive examination of the conditions, including various tests on the water, but could find nothing amiss. He also interviewed every member of the staff. Just for once, Graham Young resisted the temptation to air his medical and chemical knowledge. He was cunning enough to realize that thereby he could have laid himself open to suspicion. He professed to be as totally baffled by the 'Bovingdon bug' as everyone else.

Meanwhile Biggs's condition continued to deteriorate,

and he was transferred to the National Hospital for Nervous Diseases in Queen's Square, London, where he died on 19 November. When Mr Foster received the news he dictated a memo which was circulated among all the staff informing them of the event. Graham Young took his copy to Mrs Smart, who was later to say that 'he looked very hot and tense and was in a state of extreme animation. He told me he couldn't cope with his work and asked me to help him with it'. This she did, packing export orders and entering them in the despatch daybook, while Graham paced back and forth. 'Poor old Fred,' he kept saying. 'I wonder what was wrong?'

Panic reigned at Hadland's, especially since Dr Hynd had pronounced the factory clear of any infection. Many employees threatened to quit, and nobody could blame them. John Hadland, the chairman, who had recently returned from a lengthy business trip abroad, called in a local doctor, Dr Iain Anderson, who acted as the firm's medical officer, to come and give the staff a pep-talk. He came the same afternoon and addressed the entire staff, who were assembled in the canteen.

The various theories were all examined and one by one discarded. There was, he said, no question of radioactive contamination from the disused airfield. An analysis of the water showed that it was not contaminated by anything. Heavy metal poisoning was the next theory. Thallium was used industrially in the manufacture of high-refractive index lenses such as those made by Hadland's, but, curiously enough, Hadland's did not use this substance in the manufacture of their lenses, and no thallium had ever been stocked by the firm, either now or in the past. The firm's entire stock of chemicals had been checked by him personally. What he had not checked, of course, was the contents of Graham Young's pockets!

This now left the supposed virus, the so-called 'Bovingdon bug'. There can be no other explanation, Dr Anderson averred. The 'bug' was striking in a particularly virulent form, and no stone was being left unturned in the efforts being made to trace the source of this contamination. He was confident that the solution would soon be forthcoming. Dr Anderson took his seat, and Mr Hadland asked the assembled staff if anyone had any questions.

There was a pregnant silence. Then a voice spoke up from the back row. 'Why has heavy metal poisoning been ruled out? Weren't the symptoms all consistent with those of heavy metal poisoning?' The speaker warmed to his subject as he went into great detail of the kind usually found only in medical textbooks. This cause had been too hastily ruled out, he said. It was Graham Young.

Dr Anderson, who had a private suspicion that this was indeed so, was alarmed. He did not wish to panic the staff and was trying to play down the whole thing. He told the speaker that what the visiting experts had said was the basis of their conclusions, hoping that this would satisfy him. But Young refused to be put off. 'But were the symptoms suffered by those who were ill any different from those of the two men who died?' he persisted. 'There was no reason to suppose so,' Anderson replied. He felt far from convinced that he was right, but somehow he must shut this fellow up before the implications of his questioning sent shock-waves of apprehension through the workforce.

'But what about the alopecia [baldness]? Are you seriously suggesting that alopecia can be psychosomatic?'

Anderson fended off the question, but there was no stopping Young once he had launched into a discourse on his favourite subject. As he described in minute detail the damage that can be done to the neurological system by metallic poisons, Anderson looked at Hadland with a silent plea that he would somehow declare this meeting closed. Things were getting out of hand. Hadland declared, looking at his watch, that time was running out and that Dr Anderson had another appointment.

After the meeting, Dr Anderson followed Young into the stores department. He knew that this man was well-informed and up to date with the latest medical questions, including the controversial one about the possibility of alopecia having a psychosomatic cause which had been the subject of lengthy discussion in *The Lancet* and other medical journals. Dr Anderson began by complimenting Young on his extensive medical and chemical knowledge. Drawing him out further, he realized that Young's knowledge of poisons, and metallic poisons in particular, far exceeded his own. He had a nagging gut feeling that there was more to the so-called 'Bovingdon bug' than met the eye.

As soon as he decently could, Dr Anderson left Young and hastened to seek out John Hadland, who told him that their young medical and chemical expert had been recommended to them by the Government occupational training centre in Slough and that he had been given to understand that Young had been in a mental hospital at one stage for a nervous breakdown. No, he had no idea which mental hospital he had been in. But he decided that it might be a good idea to go into his background. Dr Anderson's comments had sown the seeds of suspicion in his mind. But it was pure speculation – nothing more. He had no evidence that anyone had been deliberately poisoned. He rang his solicitor for advice. The solicitor told him that there would be no harm in discreetly informing the police that since two of his employees had died and several more had been, and indeed still were, seriously ill, all within a fairly short space of time, he was wondering whether there could possibly be an element of foul play involved. Since he had no concrete evidence against anybody, the solicitor advised, he should request an interview with a senior officer and ask his advice.

Detective Chief Inspector John Kirkpatrick, from Hemel Hempstead police station, was detailed to call on Mr Hadland, who outlined his employees' symptoms. Kirkpatrick asked to see the firm's employment register, and noticed immediately that the sequence of sickness, commencing with the attacks suffered by Bob Egle and Ron Hewitt, coincided with the arrival of the new storekeeper who knew so much about poisons.

Kirkpatrick told Mr Hadland that he would look into the matter personally. First of all, he had to try to obtain a book which dealt in detail with thallium poisoning, and check the symptoms outlined in the book with those which had been presented by Bob Egle, Ron Hewitt, Fred Biggs, Mrs Smart and others. Since it was the weekend, the scientific libraries were closed, and finding the requisite book was proving something of a problem. He decided to confide in Detective Chief Superintendent Ronald Harvey, the head of Hertfordshire CID. By a fortunate coincidence Harvey was attending a conference of forensic scientists at the time Kirkpatrick's call came through. Informed that the call was urgent, Harvey was called from the conference room to take the call. He agreed to try to trace a copy of the book required.

On returning to his seat at the conference table he mentioned the symptoms described by Kirkpatrick to the two men who were sitting on either side of him. One was Keith Mant, a forensic pathologist; the other was Ian Holden, a former director of the Aldermaston research establishment. Both immediately recognized the symptoms as those of thallium poisoning. Harvey was elated, and as soon as he could he left the meeting and drove straight to Hemel Hempstead to see Kirkpatrick. 'You won't need the book,' he told him. 'Keith Mant and Ian Holden both say it's thallium poisoning – and they should know!'

Harvey and Kirkpatrick summoned both Mr Hadland and Mr Foster to meet them at the county police HQ. They decided to inquire about Young at Scotland Yard who, after a search in their records, were able to inform them that Young had been released from Broadmoor only nine months earlier after being detained for more than eight years.

'Eight years?' said Kirkpatrick in utter amazement. 'That's a long time to receive treatment for a nervous breakdown!'

'Oh, is that what he told you?'

'Yes. And why Broadmoor? That's a criminal institution!'

'He was sent there after poisoning his family and a school friend. He was only fourteen at the time.'

'My God,' Kirkpatrick said. 'What did he poison them with?'

'Thallium.'

Graham Young was arrested at the home of his aunt and uncle in Sheerness at 11.30 p.m. on 20 November. He was told that he was being arrested on suspicion of murder, and handcuffed. Graham had been in the kitchen, making himself an egg sandwich, after a night out at the pub with his aunt and uncle. His aunt stood nearby. 'Oh, dear! what have you been doing now, Graham?' she said. Graham went white to the lips. 'I don't know what they're talking about,' he replied. As the officers led him away, she heard him ask them: 'Which one is it you're doing me for?' At the police-station he pestered the officers with questions. What was he supposed to have done? Suspicion of murder – whom was he suspected of murdering? Eventually the police informed him that they were making inquiries into the death of Fred Biggs.

'What's that got to do with me?' demanded Young. 'There was a virus going around. The Ministry of Health said so. Doctor Anderson said so. It was called the "Bovingdon bug". That's what Biggs died from.'

Young was searched; nothing incriminating was found on him, but it was a different matter when the three officers, Detective Sergeant Robert Livingstone, Detective Inspector John Ratcliffe and Detective Constable Michael Grinstead, visited Young's bedsitter in Maynard's Road, Hemel Hempstead. The room was festooned with pictures of Hitler and other Nazi leaders, and swastikas hung everywhere. A closet was full of bottles and phials, all containing various chemicals. These included deadly poisons such as thallium, antimony, atropine, aconitine, digitalis and others, which made a colourful but lethal display in their blue, green and brown bottles. The bookshelves displayed volumes such as *Aids to Forensic Medicine* as well as books about the First and Second World Wars, Hitler and Nazism, a German grammar and dictionary, and a diary. A number of drawings were lying around showing skulls and crossbones, poison syringes and bottles, graves and headstones, men clutching their throats with agonized faces, and 'before and after' drawings depicting men with a full head of hair and afterwards bald. These were considered to have special significance on account of the loss of hair being a symptom characteristic of thallium poisoning.

The diary proved to be most informative to the police. At first Graham maintained that the diary was merely his notes for a work of fiction, and that he was preparing to write a novel. Asked to whom the various initials referred, he said that they were the initials of the imaginary characters of his proposed novel. He admitted that the diary was his, and in his own handwriting.

At a later interview, however, Graham eventually

agreed that the initials referred to his various work-mates at Hadland's – 'F' was Fred Biggs, 'B' was Bob Egle, 'D' was David Tilson, and so on. Detective Chief Superintendent Harvey now felt that Young was ready to make a confession. He began to draw him out with questions on the more technical points of various poisons. As Young warmed to his subject he was overpowered by his irresistible compulsion to expatiate on his vast knowledge of chemicals and their properties.

'You must have studied a great deal to be so knowledgeable about these things,' said Harvey.

'Yes,' replied Young, 'I have studied chemistry and toxicology since I was twelve ... I even studied in Broadmoor. The doctors there told me I had a good chance of going to university if I continued my studies. I can now, if you like, give you a complete rundown on the effects of thallium on the human body ...' For the next twenty minutes Harvey listened, fascinated in spite of himself. 'The description he gave,' Harvey was to tell the court at Young's trial, 'was full of medical terms I had never heard of.'

'Tell me: how did you poison your work-mates?'

Young told Harvey that he gave Bob Egle eighteen grains in two doses, Fred Biggs the same amount in three doses, Jethro Batt four grains and David Tilson between five and six grains. He also gave antimony to some people 'in order to baffle the doctors'. He told of poisoning Trevor Sparkes, about whom the police had not hitherto heard. Finally, he confessed to having killed his stepmother, boasting that he had committed the perfect murder. He knew that he could not be charged with that, nor could any reference be made to his previous offences if he pleaded not guilty to the present charges.

'Tell me one thing,' Harvey continued. 'What was your motive? All these people were your friends and colleagues. Why did you do it?'

'I suppose I had ceased to see them as people – at least, a part of me had. They were simply guinea-pigs.'

While Young was in custody, intensive inquiries were continuing. Organs from Biggs' body had been sent, after the post-mortem, for scientific analysis by Nigel Fuller at the Metropolitan Police Forensic Laboratories, and Fuller had found 120 grams of thallium in the intestines, twenty micrograms in the left kidney, five in muscle samples, five in bone marrow samples and ten in brain samples. The roots of the head, pubic and axillary hair had turned black – another symptom of thallium poisoning. Six micrograms were also found in a urine sample. Since these were residual amounts, Biggs had obviously been fed much larger quantities of thallium before he died.

The next step in the establishment of the case against Graham Young was to exhume the ashes of Bob Egle, in which Fuller found nine milligrams of thallium. When Young was eventually charged with Bob Egle's murder, it was the first time in criminal history that a murder charge had followed the exhumation of cremated ashes.

It was also Nigel Fuller who analysed the contents of the phials and bottles found in Young's room. More than 434 milligrams of thallium were found, among other substances. These included a bottle containing 32.33 grams of antimony – more than 200 times a fatal dose.

After a number of preliminary hearings at which various additional charges were added to the indictment and a solicitor was appointed for him by the court, the date was set for his trial, which opened on 19 July 1972 at St Albans' Crown Court before Mr Justice Eveleigh. Young was charged with the murders of Robert Egle and Fred Biggs, and to the attempted murders of David Tilson and Jethro Batt. He was also charged with causing grievous bodily harm by the administration of poison to Trevor Sparkes, Ron Hewitt, Peter Buck and Diana Smart. The same charge was also preferred regarding Batt and Tilson as an alternative to attempted murder. Young pleaded not guilty, thus ensuring a protracted trial with the maximum publicity: he was not going to be fooled again by his solicitor into pleading guilty as he had done in 1962, whereby he had found his trial all over in ten minutes! He now looked round the court at the battery of Press reporters and photographers, the milling public in the gallery, the judge and jury, the counsel of both sides and the seventy-five witnesses, and it was quite clear to everyone who saw him that he was revelling in the publicity.

Knowing that the evidence would put paid to any

chance of his acquittal, Young played the stage for all he was worth, showing off his great knowledge of chemicals and the medical effects of poisons, but never once admitting that he had actually poisoned anyone. He was skilled in adroitly side-stepping the prosecutor's questions, and fended off any attempts to trap him with searching counter-questions which frequently had even experienced counsel hard put to it to answer in a manner which did not set them at a disadvantage.

Young's counsel, Sir Arthur Irvine, made a crucial point of his defence in pointing out that a guilty man would be most unlikely to have stood up and paraded his knowledge in the way Young did at the meeting when Dr Anderson addressed the staff of Hadland's, knowing that would inevitably draw attention to himself and to his knowledge of heavy metal poisons. He argued further that because a man had an interest in pharmacology and toxicology, that did not prove that he was guilty of poisoning his work-mates. His client had never attempted to conceal this interest, Sir Arthur continued, and in fact he was at pains to mention it on his application form when he was applying for the position in Hadland's.

But Sir Arthur knew he was on a losing wicket. He and his client had a formidable array of no fewer than seventy-five prosecution witnesses to contend with. The defence they put up was a valiant one, the best they could come up with, but it was no match for the forensic evidence which had proved beyond all possible doubt that Biggs and Egle had met their deaths from thallium poisoning and that this had occurred while they were at work, and that since Hadland's did not use thallium in their manufacturing processes then it must have been introduced from outside. All the symptoms had occurred after the victims had partaken of tea or coffee prepared by Young, and the same symptoms had attacked at least four other employees, subject of the lesser charges, who had also partaken of tea or coffee prepared by Young.

What Sir Arthur probably did not know, however, was that many murderers of this type, especially multiple murderers, have an irresistible compulsion to talk about their methods, or even the actual murders, either directly or indirectly. To the psychiatrist this is, of course, a well-known phenomenon, but Sir Arthur was not a psychiatrist – he was a barrister. Had he been aware of this facet of Young's personality, it is conceivable that he would have sought to play down rather than to highlight it in his defence arguments. It is almost as though the murderer subconsciously wishes to be caught by this obsessional revealing of the compulsive forces which drive him relentlessly to self-destruction. To give only one example, the process whereby the ashes of a cremated body could now be analysed had not been known at the time when Young had murdered his stepmother, and no one could have connected him with her death until he himself bragged about 'his perfect murder' to the police of his own volition after he had been arrested for the Hadland's crimes.

The jury took less than an hour to arrive at a unanimous verdict of guilty of the murders of Bob Egle and Fred Biggs and guilty of causing grievous bodily harm by administering poison to Ron Hewitt and Diana Smart. The charges relating to Trevor Sparkes and Peter Buck were found to be insufficiently substantiated by the available evidence, and Young was acquitted on these charges. The alternative charges relating to Jethro Batt and David Tilson were dropped.

The judge sentenced Young to life imprisonment on the two murder charges and five years on each of the other two charges, to run consecutively but concurrently with the life sentence. Before he was taken to Wormwood Scrubs (later to be transferred to Parkhurst, the maximum security prison on the Isle of Wight), the foreman of the jury asked the judge's permission to make a statement on the jury's behalf, which was granted. The foreman then read out a prepared statement: 'The members of the jury in this case consider it to be our duty to draw the attention of the authorities concerned to the failings of the present system by which poisons are sold to the public. We urge that the system be reviewed in order that in future the public may be more consistently safeguarded.' The judge thanked the jury for their attention to this matter.

After the verdict, it was now the turn of Sir Arthur Irvine to ask the judge's permission to make a statement, in which he said he believed it to be his duty to point out